Vegetation Community Monitoring at Cumberland Island National Seashore, 2009

Natural Resource Report NPS/SECN/NRDS—2012/260

Michael W. Byrne and Sarah L. Corbett

USDI National Park Service
Southeast Coast Inventory and Monitoring Network
Cumberland Island National Seashore
101 Wheeler Street
Saint Marys, Georgia, 31558

and

Joseph C. DeVivo

USDI National Park Service
Southeast Coast Inventory and Monitoring Network
University of Georgia
160 Phoenix Road, Phillips Lab
Athens, Georgia, 30605

March 2012

U.S. Department of the Interior
National Park Service
Natural Resource Stewardship and Science
Fort Collins, Colorado

The National Park Service, Natural Resource Stewardship and Science office in Fort Collins, Colorado publishes a range of reports that address natural resource topics of interest and applicability to a broad audience in the National Park Service and others in natural resource management, including scientists, conservation and environmental constituencies, and the public.

The Natural Resource Data Series is intended for the timely release of basic data sets and data summaries. Care has been taken to assure accuracy of raw data values, but a thorough analysis and interpretation of the data has not been completed. Consequently, the initial analyses of data in this report are provisional and subject to change.

All manuscripts in the series receive the appropriate level of peer review to ensure that the information is scientifically credible, technically accurate, appropriately written for the intended audience, and designed and published in a professional manner.

This report received informal peer review by subject-matter experts who were not directly involved in the collection, analysis, or reporting of the data.

Data in this report were collected and analyzed using methods based on established, peer-reviewed protocols and were analyzed and interpreted within the guidelines of the protocols.

Views, statements, findings, conclusions, recommendations, and data in this report do not necessarily reflect views and policies of the National Park Service, U.S. Department of the Interior. Mention of trade names or commercial products does not constitute endorsement or recommendation for use by the U.S. Government.

This report is available from (http://science.nature.nps.gov/im/units/secn) and the Natural Resource Publications Management website (http://www.nature.nps.gov/publications/nrpm/).

Please cite this publication as:

Byrne, M. W., S. L. Corbett, and J. C. DeVivo. 2012. Vegetation community monitoring at Cumberland Island National Seashore, 2009. Natural Resource Data Series NPS/SECN/NRDS—2012/260. National Park Service, Fort Collins, Colorado.

NPS 640/112995, March 2012

Contents

Figures

Tables

List of Terms

Absolute cover: The total amount of ground surface that is covered by each species or group. Describes the amount of cover that each species or group represents in a stratum. Expressed as a percentage. Can exceed 100% due to overlap. The total cover of each species or group divided by the total possible cover for a plot.

Canopy species: Woody species known to occur in the midstory or overstory of the canopy, or shrub species that grow greater than or equal to 4 cm DBH and measureable at breast height (1.4 m).

Canopy stratum: The structural zone above 1.1 m (i.e., elbow height of a typical observer as per densiometer instructions) and consists of all live and dead plant material that affects the amount of light penetrating to the ground. This includes individual elements whose cover is also potentially measured and accounted for in the shrub- or groundcover-stratum measurements, but exceeds 1.1 m in height, is detected by the densiometer, and contributes to canopy cover. Also referred to as the midstory, overstory, or sub-canopy.

Cover: The vertical projection of the outermost extent of a species, or the extent of the shadow cast by the species if the sun were directly overhead. Foliar cover.

DBH: Diameter at breast height, or 1.4 m above the ground's surface.

Frequency: The number of times a species or group is detected in a plot, expressed as a percentage. Provides information on regularity at which a species or group is encountered.

Groundcover stratum: The structural zone that consists of all non-woody species (i.e., forbs and graminoids), and all woody species (i.e., shrubs and trees) with a DBH of less than 1 cm and seedlings 30 cm or less in height.

Relative cover: The cover of each species or group as a function of all other plant species that occurred in a plot. Describes the percentage of cover that each species represents out of the total vegetative cover in a stratum. Expressed as a percentage. Always sums to 100%. The total cover of each species or group divided by the sum of the cover of all other species that occur in a plot.

Seedlings: Woody dicotyledonous plants less than 30 cm in height.

Shrub stratum: All woody species greater than 30 cm in height with a DBH of 1–4 cm.

Stratum: A structural size category of vegetation at a site. These are the canopy, shrub, and groundcover layers.

Executive Summary

In 2009, the National Park Service (NPS) Southeast Coast Network (SECN) Inventory and Monitoring Network began collecting vegetation community data as part the NPS Vital Signs monitoring program. Information collected under this Vital Sign will be used to help managers make better informed decisions by understanding trends and variability related to plant species, frequency of occurrence, percent cover, diversity, and distribution in the groundcover, shrub, and canopy strata.

Within each stratum, vegetation communities were sampled using a hybrid of methods used by the North Carolina Vegetation Survey nested-subplot design (Peet et al. 1998) within a circular plot similar to the Forest Inventory and Analysis protocol (Bechtold and Patterson 2005). This report summarizes vegetation community data collected at Cumberland Island National Seashore in 2009.

1. Data were collected at 30 spatially-balanced random locations at the Seashore. The findings below apply only to portions of the park that meet the following site selection criteria:

    a) Sites are located within park boundaries and ownership.

    b) Sites must be sampleable within safety guidelines.

    c) Sites cannot be located in wholly non-natural areas, open water, or areas where application of the methods is inappropriate (such as marshes).

2. Sampling activities occurred at the Seashore from 9/07/2009 to 9/12/2009, 9/21/2009 to 9/30/2009, and 10/8/2009 to 10/12/2009

3. Monitoring efforts resulted in the addition of five species, subspecies, or varieties to the park's species list.

4. Absolute canopy cover across the park was approximately 75%.

5. Laurel oak (*Quercus laurifolia*) had the largest average diameter at breast height of any canopy species at the park.

6. Redbay (*Persea borbonia*) seedlings were detected at a frequency of $0.16/m^2$.

7. Saw palmetto (*Serenoa repens*) was the most frequently occurring species in the shrub stratum.

8. Live redbay occurred in 50% of shrub plots.

9. *Dichanthelium* spp., unknown Asteraceae seedlings, and rusty lyonia (*Lyonia ferruginea*) were the most frequently occurring species/elements in the groundcover stratum.

10. Saw palmetto had the highest absolute and relative cover in the shrub stratum.

11. Muscadine grape (*Vitis rotundifolia*) had the highest relative cover, and Sand cordgrass (*Spartina bakeri*) had the highest absolute cover in the groundcover stratum.

12. The full dataset, and associated metadata, can be acquired from the data store at http://science.nature.nps.gov/nrdata/

Introduction

Overview

Vegetation communities provide many ecosystem services. Among their many functions, they are an important component of food webs and wildlife habitat for many species, and serve as a carbon sink, produce oxygen, cycle nutrients and energy through an ecosystem, influence the local climate, improve water quality, and moderate flooding and erosion. Plant communities also respond to multiple stressors such as changes in air quality, hydrology, disturbance regimes, and climate. Determining trends in vegetation communities is vital to understanding the ecological processes occurring at a site, and identifying stressors and their impacts.

Vegetation communities are dynamic entities with constant changes in composition, cover, distribution, and structure that reflect stressor response, natural or anthropogenic in origin. Disturbance is the primary stressor and regulating mechanism of SECN vegetation communities. The timing, type, and extent of the disturbance generally evoke a distinguishable response in the species composition, diversity, and structure of the landscape (Foster et al. 1998, Turner et al. 1990). The primary natural-disturbance processes in SECN parks are fire and weather (e.g., hurricanes, drought). Anthropogenic influences include fire suppression, landscape fragmentation, altered hydrology, and non-native species introduction.

The SECN is composed of a diverse assemblage of vegetation communities. Approximately 180 vegetation associations (i.e., fine-resolution floristic description), as defined by the National Vegetation and Classification System (FGDC 2008), occur in the SECN. These communities vary widely in distribution, species composition, and structure, and include sparsely vegetated primary dune communities, late successional old-growth bottomland hardwood forest communities, and highly diverse herbaceous-dominated mesic pine savannah communities.

Given the widespread anthropogenic influences in SECN parks and the importance of vegetation communities, quantifying trends in plant cover, frequency, diversity, and distribution is a high priority (DeVivo et al. 2008). Evaluating trends in these metrics provides measures for assessing the ecological integrity and sustainability of southeastern ecosystems, and identifying the need for specific management activities on our park lands. The National Park Service Omnibus Management Act of 1998, and other reinforcing policies and regulations, require park managers "to establish baseline information and to provide information on the long-term trends in the condition of National Park System resources" (Title II, Sec. 204). The vegetation-community monitoring data summarized herein is a tool to assist park managers in fulfilling this mandate.

This report summarizes data collected as a part of the SECN's Vegetation Community Vital Signs monitoring efforts.

Monitoring Objective

- Determine trends in plant species frequency, percent cover, diversity, and distribution in the groundcover, shrub, and canopy strata.

Methods

Study Area

Cumberland Island National Seashore (CUIS), a 26-km (17.5 mile) long barrier island, is one of the larger and most diverse islands on the Atlantic Coast (Figure 1). Located off the southern Georgia coast adjacent to the Georgia-Florida border, it totals 14,743 ha (36,415 ac), of which 6,821 ha (16,850 ac) are estuarine. A cordgrass (*Spartina* spp.) dominated salt-marsh, oyster mud flats, and tidal creeks provide habitat for a diverse assemblage of fish and wildlife. The terrestrial areas of the park consist of Virginia live oak (*Quercus virginiana*)/palmetto (*Sabal palmetto*) maritime forests, extensive dune systems, interdunal wetlands, freshwater ponds and wetlands, and mixed-pine/hardwood forests in the northern part of the park. Approximately 4,000 ha (9,886 ac) of the island's northern portion are designated a Wilderness area. The coastal maritime hammock at CUIS is an excellent example of this community type and is host to a variety of resident and migratory fauna. Although many of the freshwater wetlands and pine communities on the island evolved with frequent fires that maintained an open and highly diverse understory community, the island has experienced substantial anthropogenically-influenced fire suppression over the last century. This has resulted in woody-encroachment and drying freshwater wetlands and a reduction in the diversity and composition of the herbaceous understory in the fire-adapted uplands.

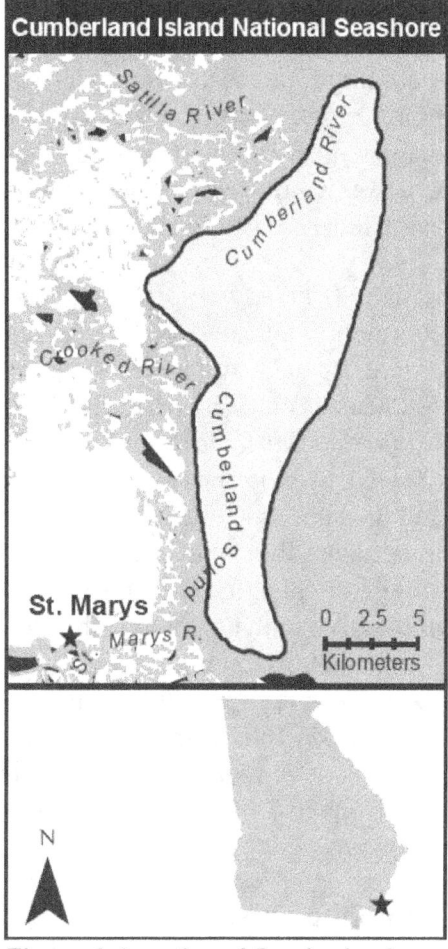

Figure 1. Location of Cumberland Island National Seashore.

The island is known as one of the primary loggerhead sea turtle nesting sites and provides key habitat for nesting and migratory shorebirds and landbirds. The island is also host to an actively controlled feral hog population and a currently uncontrolled feral horse population. Rooting by hogs, especially in wetland areas, is very destructive and seriously impedes seedling recruitment, damages groundcover, causes substantial soil disturbance, and serves as a vector for non-native plant species. Feral horses graze extensively in open areas, particularly influencing salt marshes (D. Hoffman, pers. comm.). Annual horse counts have shown little fluctuation in the horse population over the past decade (CUIS Annual Horse Count, unpublished data).

The island has a multi-century history of Native American habitation, shifting occupation by several colonial European nations, use of the island as a plantation in the early to mid-19th century, and a brief occupancy in the late 19th century by wealthy American families who used the island as their primary residence or as a winter retreat. The island is sparsely developed and many of the structures occur in the island's five historic districts listed on the National Register of Historic Places. Historic land uses have changed the vegetation communities of CUIS over the past 150 years. For instance, large live oaks from the island's interior maritime hammocks were harvested for the shipbuilding industry near the turn of the century, thus removing the largest and oldest trees from the island. The indigo, rice, and cotton plantations established during the 19th century influenced the vegetation composition and structure of forested areas and wetlands on the island. Further, loblolly pine (*Pinus taeda*) plantations were planted for silvicultural purposes. These stands replaced the native maritime hammock forests and some persist on the island.

CUIS has 790 known vascular-plant species, subspecies, and varieties (NPSpecies 2011), including five species, subspecies, and varieties added to the species list based on these monitoring efforts (Table 2, Appendix A). Non-native species present in the park that are a management challenge include Japanese and Chinese privet (*Ligustrum japonicum* and *L. sinense*), Chinaberry (*Melia azedarach*), bamboo (*Bambusa* spp.), tamarisk (*Tamarix gallica*), and Chinese wisteria (*Wisteria sinensis*).

Redbay (*Persea borbonia*) are a critical native element of the coastal maritime hammock community and also serve as an important habitat component for many vertebrates, invertebrates, vascular plants, and non-vascular plants. Occurrences of native redbay throughout coastal southeastern U.S. are in rapid decline due to the introduction of a fungal pathogen, laurel wilt (*Raffaelea lauricola*), whose vector is the non-native redbay ambrosia beetle (from Asia) (*Xyleborus glabratus*). Since the beetle's initial detection in 2002 (Haack 2006, Rabaglia 2003), and the subsequent lethality of laurel wilt to redbay, this pathogen has had a profound adverse effect on redbay in over 60 counties in the southeastern U.S. (Fraedrich et al. 2008), primarily along the Atlantic coast (http://www.fs.fed.us/r8/foresthealth/laurelwilt/dist_map.shtml). The non-native redbay ambrosia beetle, and laurel wilt, does occur at CUIS, and has caused an estimated 90% mortality of redbay over 4 cm in diameter at the park (J. Fry, pers. comm.). Extensive multi-agency efforts are currently underway to further understand this pathogen, identify possible methods of eradication, and identify mitigation procedures to ensure the persistence of redbay and other potentially susceptible members of the Lauraceae. The breadth of the adverse ecological impacts of the loss of redbay in the coastal maritime hammock is unknown.

Sampling Design

To allow for park-wide inference, the park's administrative boundary was used as the sampling frame, which was divided into a systematic 0.5-ha grid; the center point of each grid cell served as the potential sampling site and the grid cell served as the macroplot. A spatially-balanced sample was drawn from this grid using the Reversed Randomized Quadrant-Recursive Raster (RRQRR) algorithm (Theobald et al. 2007). Alternate points were used when selection criteria (i.e., including safety and access issues) were not met. A sample size of 30 was chosen after consideration of park size, hypothesized variability, and logistical issues regarding travel time and conducting monitoring activities in five to six park units per year. The Seashore was sampled from 9/07/2009 to 9/12/2009, 9/21/2009 to 9/30/2009, and 10/8/2009 to 10/12/2009.

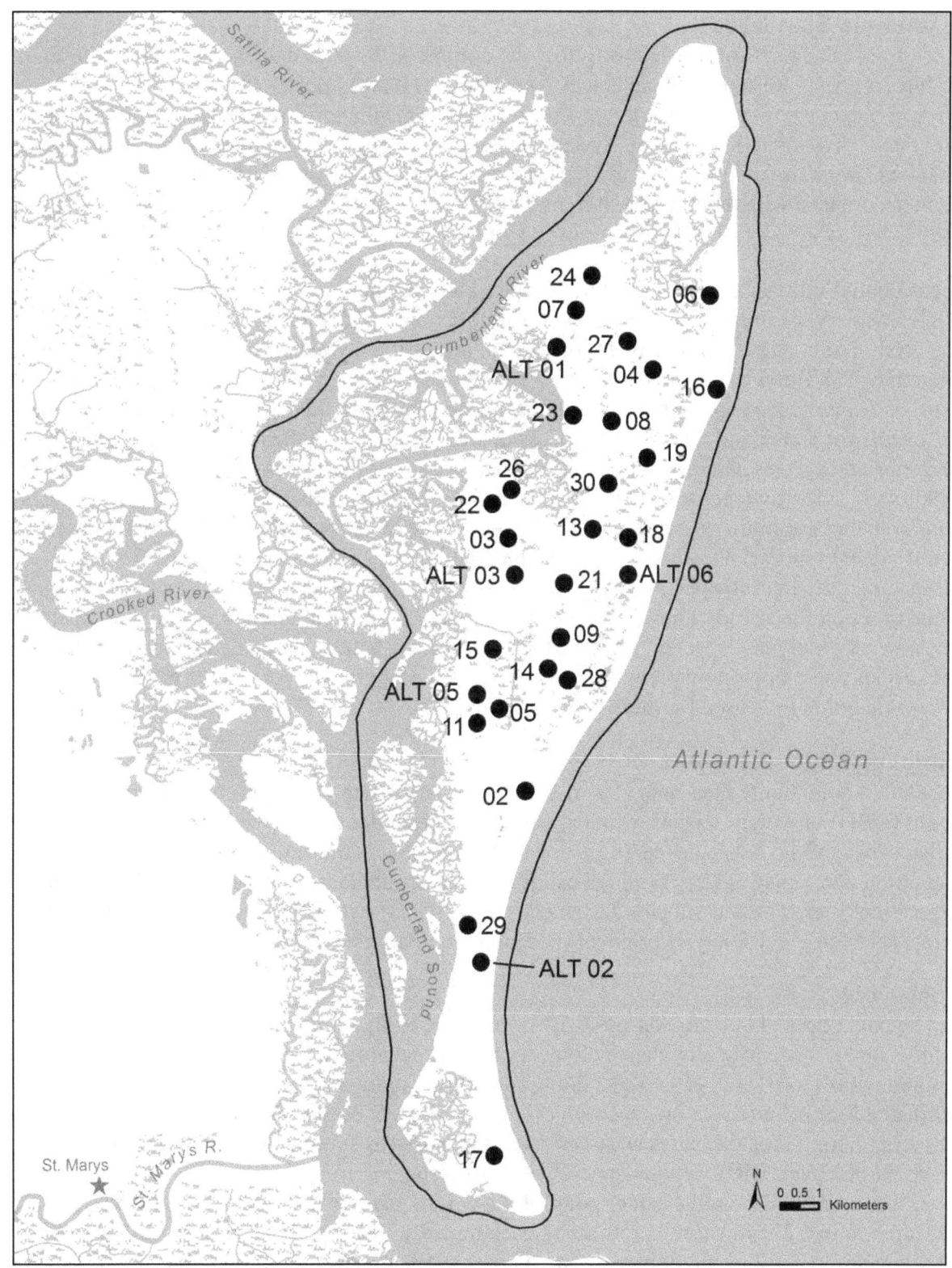

Figure 2. Spatially-balanced random sampling locations at Cumberland Island National Seashore, 2009.

Taxonomic Standards

Species nomenclature for this report follow the current NPSpecies database accessible through the Integration of Resource Management Applications (IRMA) portal (https://irma.nps.gov/App/Portal/Home), which represents the most recent updates from the Integrated Taxonomic Information System (ITIS; http://www.itis.gov). Standards used for the botanical taxonomy in this report and for all work conducted by the Southeast Coast Network are in accordance with those set forth in by ITIS (http://irma.nps.gov/content/help/taxonomy/FAQ.aspx).

Occasionally, if the available characteristics of a plant did not facilitate identification to genus, species, variety, or subspecies, the lowest level of taxonomy identifiable (i.e., the most refined) was used. For example, species of *Dicanthelium* are extremely difficult to identify to species when they lack floral or fruiting structures. In this case, the specimen may only be identified to genus as *Dicanthelium* sp. In the event that a species has more than one variety or subspecies that occurs for a park and the specific variety or subspecies cannot be identified in the field, only the genus and species name were used. For example, several varieties of *Pteridium aquilinum* are known. If for some reason the observer was only able to identify the plant as *Pteridium aquilinum* and not further to variety, only *Pteridium aquilinum* was reported. In these cases, the identified and reported name may not be included in the existing park species list from NPSpecies, only the sub-species or varieties are included in the park species list. Because the genus or species is already known to occur in the park, the general taxonomy will not appear in the "new vascular plant species" (Table 2). In the event a family name, generic name, or genera and species name only (no variety, subspecies, etc.) is used, the most recent taxonomy represented in ITIS is used for these general terms.

Sampling Methodology

Vegetation community measures were divided into three strata based upon diameter at breast height (DBH) of woody species: canopy, shrub, and groundcover. Any non-woody (i.e., herbaceous) species was considered part of the groundcover stratum. Within each stratum, vegetation communities were sampled using a hybrid of methods used by the North Carolina Vegetation Survey nested-subplot design (Peet et al. 1998) within a circular plot similar to the Forest Inventory and Analysis protocol (Bechtold and Patterson 2005).

Plot Layout

The layout consisted of a circular plot with a radius of 15 m within the 0.5-ha macroplot. Subplots were systematically placed along six transects that radiated out from the center point at azimuths of 0°/360°, 60°, 120°, 180°, 240°, and 300° (Figure 3). To avoid overlap, subplots originated four meters from the macroplot (i.e., 0.5-ha grid) center point and extended away from the center point. Five measures were collected in the nested subplots within each plot: canopy cover, shrub cover, DBH, canopy-species seedling frequency, and herbaceous cover. Canopy cover was measured from the center point of the 0.5-ha macroplot. Shrub coverage was measured in two 2 × 4 m shrub plots along each transect. The shrub plots were further subdivided into 2 × 2 m subplots to improve cover-estimation accuracy and precision because cover-estimation error increases with plot size (solid gray shading, Figure 3). Groundcover coverage, groundcover nested frequency, and seedling frequency was measured in two 1 × 1 m groundcover plots (solid black shading, Figure 3) along each transect. Canopy species DBH was measured in three sections, each representing 1/3 of the total circular plot (hashed gray shading, Figure 3).

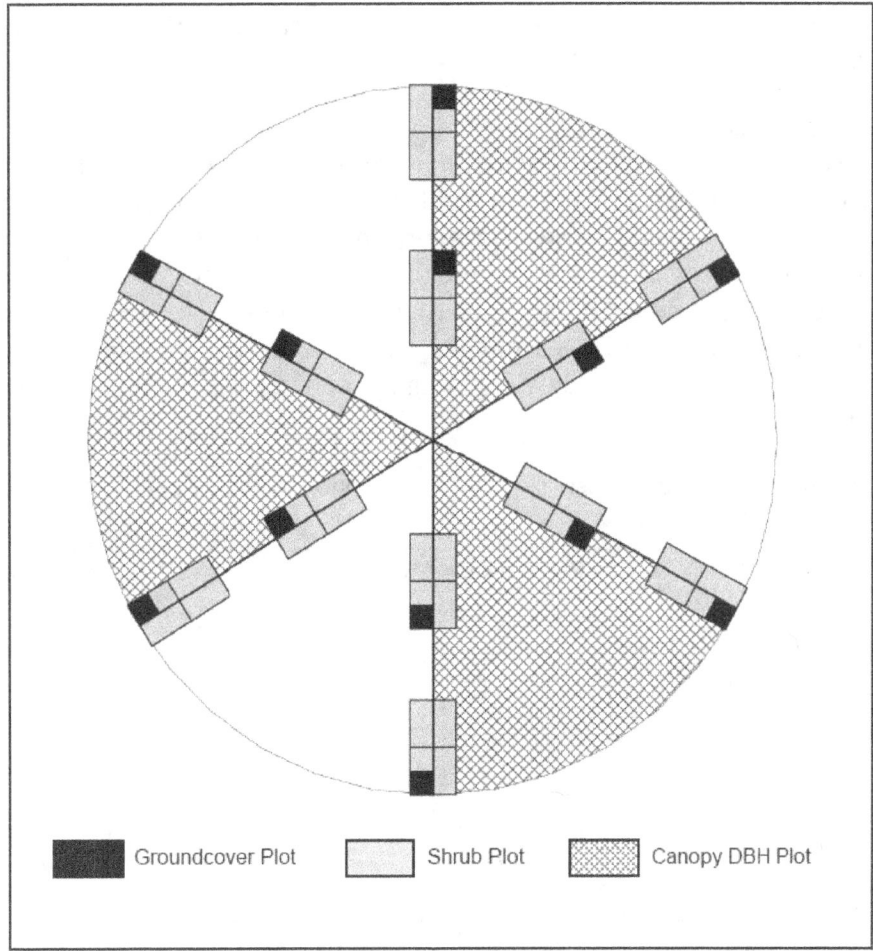

Groundcover Plot   Shrub Plot   Canopy DBH Plot

Figure 3. Southeast Coast Network vegetation-community monitoring plot layout.

Canopy Measures
Absolute canopy cover was estimated in the four cardinal directions with a concave spherical densiometer placed on a 1.1-m tall tripod at the plot center. Canopy cover reported is the mean of three observers across the four cardinal directions. The circular plot was subdivided into six sections occurring between the 0–60°, 120–180°, and 240–300° compass transects of the circular plot. Diameter at breast height (i.e., 1.37 m above the ground) was measured to the nearest millimeter for all trees (identified by species) with a diameter greater than or equal to 4 cm that occur within the 0–60°, 120–180°, and 240–300° section.

Shrub Measures
Shrub cover of all shrub species was visually estimated for each of the twelve 2 × 4 m plots. A common source of error in visual estimation of vegetation cover is that as plot size increases, cover-estimation error increases. Each shrub plot was therefore sub-divided into two 2 × 2 m subplots. The plots are situated at 15 m and 8 m (extending toward the plot center) along each of the transect lines of the circular plot. Shrub cover was categorized into one of seven coverage classes (Table 1) for each subplot. A coverage class of zero (Table 1) is assumed for any shrub

species not detected and not recorded on the datasheet. The measurements of subplots were combined by averaging the midpoint for the coverage class in the two shrub subplots resulting in a total shrub cover estimate for the 2 × 4 m plot. The authors have established consistent performance in the accuracy and precision of visual-cover estimates within and across observers in plots this size.

Groundcover Measures

Groundcover was visually estimated in each of the twelve 1 × 1 m plots situated on the clockwise side at 15 m and 8 m (extending toward the plot center) along each of the transect lines of the circular plot. Groundcover was categorized into one of seven coverage classes (Table 1) for each plot. A coverage class of zero (Table 1) is assumed for any groundcover species not detected and not recorded on the datasheet. The authors have established through trials that these coverage classes are discriminatory and repeatable across observers. Canopy-species seedling counts were estimated by counting the number of seedlings that occur in each of the 1 × 1 m plots.

Table 1. Cover estimation coverage class, percent cover range, and value used for analyses for SECN vegetation-community monitoring protocol.

Coverage Class	Percent Cover Range	Value Used for Analyses
0	0%	0.0
1	Trace (<1%)	0.5
2	1-5%	2.5
3	5-25%	15.0
4	25-50%	37.5
5	50-75%	62.5
6	75-95%	85.0
7	95-100%	97.5

Data Analysis

Because this is the first year of this protocol's implementation at the Seashore, only the status of the elements presented in the aforementioned monitoring objective are determined; except diversity and distribution. The data in this report are presented by plot and pooled across plots. Sampling locations are presented in Figure 2 and summaries by plot are presented in Tables 3–9.

Summaries include (a) new species detected (Table 2),(b) canopy cover (Table 3), (c) canopy species size (Table 4), (d) seedling frequency (Table 5), (e) shrub species relative cover and frequency (Table 6), shrub species absolute cover and frequency (Table 7), (f) groundcover relative cover and frequency (Table 8), (g) groundcover absolute cover and frequency (Table 9), and (h) species detected (Appendix A).

Findings

We detected 101 species, subspecies, and varieties during this monitoring effort (Appendix A), including five new species, subspecies, and varieties not previously known to occur at the Seashore (Table 2).

Table 2. New vascular plant species detected at Cumberland Island National Seashore during 2009 monitoring efforts and recommended NPSpecies classifications.

Species	Abundance	Nativity	Pest	Management Priority	Exploitation Concerns
Andropogon virginicus var. virginicus	Unknown	Native	No	No	No
Aristida stricta	Unknown	Native	No	No	No
Lyonia fruticosa	Unknown	Native	No	No	No
Rhynchospora latifolia	Unknown	Native	No	No	No
Rhynchospora megalocarpa	Unknown	Native	No	No	No

Measures of Community Structure

Absolute canopy cover was variable across the all sampling locations at the park ($\bar{x} = 74.78\%$, SD = 21.8; Table 3). The largest tree detected was a laurel oak (*Quercus laurifolia*; 130.2 cm), and laurel oak had the largest average DBH ($\bar{x} = 48.71$ cm, SD = 23.97) of any species where more than ten individuals were sampled (Table 4). One live redbay (*Persea borbonia*) was detected, having a DBH of 9.1 cm. Standing dead redbay DBH averaged 14.63 cm (SD = 8.01). Forty-seven canopy-sized dead redbay were identified within the sampling plots parkwide. Redbay seedlings were estimated at a frequency of $0.16/m^2$ (Table 5). Live redbay occurred in the shrub stratum in 50% of sampling locations (Table 6). Saw palmetto (*Serenoa repens*) was the most frequently occurring shrub species at the park ($f = 76.67$) and had the highest relative cover of all other shrub species ($\bar{x} = 36.05\%$, SD = 33.23; Table 6). Saw palmetto also had the highest absolute cover ($\bar{x} = 26.27\%$, SD = 29.92; Table 7). *Dichanthelium* spp. was the most frequently occurring element (63.33%) in the groundcover stratum (Table 8). Unknown Asteraceae (sunflower family) seedlings were the next most frequent element (53.33%), and rusty fetterbush (*Lyonia ferruginea*) was the third most frequent element (43.33%). Muscadine grape (*Vitis rotundifolia*) had the highest relative cover in the groundcover stratum ($\bar{x} = 1.83\%$, SD = 3.6; Table 8). Sand cordgrass (*Spartina bakeri*) had the highest absolute cover in the groundcover stratum ($\bar{x} = 2.49\%$, SD = 13.42) followed by the non-native centipedegrass (*Eremochloa ophiuroides*) spp. ($\bar{x} = 2.28\%$, SD = 6.26; Table 9).

Table 3. Average canopy cover in vegetation monitoring sampling locations at Cumberland Island National Seashore, 2009.

Sampling Location	Average Canopy Cover	Standard Deviation
CUIS-2	68.33	3.88
CUIS-3	92.83	2.52
CUIS-4	94.08	0.72
CUIS-5	48.33	4.26
CUIS-6	88.67	0.58
CUIS-7	63.92	2.4
CUIS-8	81.88	1.89
CUIS-9	83.58	2.24
CUIS-11	93.5	1
CUIS-13	81.5	3.07
CUIS-14	41.42	0.14
CUIS-15	82.33	1.38
CUIS-16	61.58	2.08
CUIS-17	0.08	0.14
CUIS-18	64.83	0.52
CUIS-19	64.69	3.38
CUIS-21	79.67	0.14
CUIS-22	28.42	4.01
CUIS-23	91.58	0.14
CUIS-24	92.25	0.66
CUIS-26	90	2.05
CUIS-27	69.25	5.58
CUIS-28	80.58	1.46
CUIS-29	91.58	0.76
CUIS-30	91.25	N/A
CUIS-A1	90.33	2.9
CUIS-A2	90.42	1.28
CUIS-A3	66.25	1.95
CUIS-A5	86.42	2.89
CUIS-A6	83.75	2.17
Park Average	**74.78**	**21.8**

Table 4. Average canopy species size, measured as diameter (cm) at breast height (DBH) for species sampled in vegetation monitoring sampling locations at Cumberland Island National Seashore, 2009. Numbers in parentheses indicate the number of individual trees measured within each plot.

Species	Avg	Std Dev	Sampling Point																													
			2	3	4	5	6	7	8	9	11	13	14	15	16	17	18	19	21	22	23	24	26	27	28	29	30	A1	A2	A3	A5	A6
Cephalanthus occidentalis	5.48	1.32																															5.48 (4)
Ilex cassine	6.43	1.7																															6.43 (3)
Ilex opaca	17.89	6.57	19.81 (9)					24.70 (2)	30.10 (1)		18.87 (3)			17.40 (1)						15.20 (1)		15.35 (10)					13.90 (1)				15.67 (6)	
Juniperus virginiana	6.05	1.48		6.05 (2)																													
Lyonia ferruginea	7.51	3.01	7.72 (9)	7.16 (27)	6.24 (28)				9.80 (1)	7.80 (18)				7.15 (2)			5.30 (5)		5.85 (2)	5.65 (8)	7.34 (10)		9.78 (26)	5.30 (1)	8.00 (46)	7.10 (2)	9.80 (8)	6.76 (26)	7.40 (12)		6.67 (10)	
Lyonia lucida	4.55	0.64																								4.55 (2)							
Morella cerifera	6.48	2.25			7.10 (2)					8.25 (4)					5.60 (15)						6.10 (1)					6.30 (1)			6.33 (3)				6.78 (27)
Nyssa sylvatica var. biflora	30.80																																30.80 (1)
Osmanthus americanus	8.34	3.77			7.34 (8)											4.00 (1)										16.40 (1)							
Persea borbonia	9.10																											9.10 (1)					
Pinus elliottii	23.05	19.07					25.40 (4)		48.70 (2)		47.80 (1)	8.68 (22)		61.50 (1)				55.60 (3)	39.63 (3)	13.35 (2)										35.94 (5)		
Pinus palustris	29.60	28.51						8.80 (3)			130.20 (1)										41.60 (2)		60.80 (2)										
Pinus serotina	55.25	9.4																						55.25 (2)								
Pinus taeda	15.53	13.58	11.00 (1)	33.23 (3)		13.25 (30)				14.30 (1)	20.60 (1)	13.95 (11)	47.70 (1)	12.33 (12)						22.70 (1)										47.70 (1)		
Prunus serotina	31.90	14.33																					32.40 (2)				30.90 (1)						
Quercus geminata	11.20	5.12			11.68 (19)											8.10 (3)																
Quercus laurifolia	48.71	23.97	55.80 (2)						47.00 (1)								63.30 (1)			41.60 (2)		31.20 (3)								49.00 (1)	43.45 (8)	
Quercus myrtifolia	9.25	3.7			9.15 (20)																								9.93 (3)				
Quercus virginiana	43.98	18.43					67.00 (2)	76.30 (1)	32.00 (3)	45.47 (3)	56.85 (2)						95.90 (1)		28.53 (12)		41.96 (13)	48.50 (1)	40.80 (4)		24.40 (1)	56.80 (3)	62.23 (4)	31.30 (1)	42.83 (8)			56.75 (2)
Sabal palmetto	43.69	15.04														43.69 (9)																
Salix caroliniana	10.14	2.78													10.95 (4)																		10.02 (25)
Sideroxylon sp.	17.3	3													17.30 (1)																		
Sideroxylon tenax	14.66	4.93													14.66 (5)																		

Table 4. Continued.

Species	Avg	Std Dev	2	3	4	5	6	7	8	9	11	13	14	15	16	17	18	19	21	22	23	24	26	27	28	29	30	A1	A2	A3	A5	A6
Symplocos tinctoria	4.72	0.81																													4.70 (1)		
Vaccinium arboreum	7.32	3.14	6.43 (19)					4.65 (2)			8.09 (15)			6.49 (8)			9.87 (3)	12.43 (4)		6.91 (14)	8.07 (3)					5.92 (5)						
Vitis rotundifolia	4.97	0.74	4.80 (1)								5.50 (1)										4.68 (4)					5.10 (6)						
Dead																																
Cephalanthus occidentalis	5.88	1.16																															5.88 (4)
Ilex opaca	14.65	4.11																														14.65 (4)	
Juniperus virginiana	19.73	17.49																		9.70 (2)												39.80 (1)	
Lyonia ferruginea	6.52	1.85							9.60 (1)								6.49 (31)	5.70 (2)		5.30 (1)								5.40 (1)	8.40 (1)			
Lyonia fruticosa	5.6																5.60 (1)														
Lyonia lucida	4.3																															4.90 (2)
Morella cerifera	6.46	2.01			8.10 (1)					7.50 (1)					7.33 (3)					4.30 (1)					4.30 (1)							
Osmanthus americanus	25.5																									25.50 (1)						
Persea borbonia	14.63	8.01		29.90 (1)					26.00 (1)	18.13 (4)										13.75 (6)		15.80 (1)		25.07 (3)		12.47 (7)	23.45 (2)	14.91 (7)	9.15 (10)	11.16 (5)			
Pinus elliottii	14.8	14.94										6.20 (2)																			32.00 (1)		
Pinus taeda	4.95	1.2				4.95 (2)																											
Quercus geminata	9.8	3.68			13.13 (3)																				8.97 (12)								
Quercus laurifolia	49.95	1.48																49.95 (2)															
Quercus myrtifolia	6.24	2.44			4.23 (3)																				6.64 (13)				6.53 (3)				
Quercus sp.	24.87	6.51																					24.87 (3)										
Quercus virginiana	24.91	10.7									16.20 (1)								23.25 (2)		24.15 (2)									24.00 (1)		39.40 (1)	
Salix caroliniana	7.34	3.07																															7.34 (7)
Vaccinium arboreum	7.87	1.1									8.50 (1)									8.50 (1)						6.60 (1)						
Unidentified																																
Tracheobionta	8	2.12																			11.20 (1)			7.20 (4)								

13

Table 5. Seedling frequency for canopy and shrub species in vegetation monitoring sampling locations at Cumberland Island National Seashore, 2009.

Species Code	Total Seedlings	Seedlings/m2	Std Dev	2	3	4	5	6	7	8	9	11	13	14	15	16	17	18	19	21	22	23	24	26	27	28	29	30	A1	A2	A3	A5	A6
Carya glabra	1	0	0.02																													0.33
Decodon verticillatus	4	0.01	0.06																								0.08						
Dichanthelium sp.	1	0	0.02																														
Fimbristylis caroliniana	0	0	0						0.08								0.00																
Gaylussacia frondosa	14	0.04	0.15			0.58																			0.58								
Ilex glabra	4	0.01	0.06		0.08	0.33																											
Ilex opaca	10	0.03	0.12									0.67									0.08												
Ilex vomitoria	11	0.03	0.12					0.33									0.58																
Lyonia ferruginea	58	0.16	0.32		0.42	0.08				1.58		0.08						0.58			0.17	0.50		0.42	0.17	0.42	0.08	0.08		0.25			
Lyonia fruticosa	11	0.03	0.17																						0.92								
Lyonia lucida	37	0.1	0.33																							0.67		1.33		1.06			
Morella cerifera	38	0.11	0.24		0.17	0.17						0.67	0.83			0.83					0.08		0.17								0.25		
Persea barbonia	56	0.16	0.32		0.25	0.33						0.25						0.08		0.17		0.17				0.08	1.25	0.25		1.00	0.83		
Pinus taeda	11	0.03	0.11		0.08		0.58					0.17																			0.08		
Prunus serotina	3	0.01	0.03																				0.17				0.08						
Quercus geminata	11	0.03	0.15			0.83																			0.08								
Quercus laurifolia	123	0.34	0.96	1.17						0.83		0.08	1.83					4.92	0.42	0.25												0.75	
Quercus myrtifolia	11	0.03	0.15																										0.83				
Quercus sp.	235	0.65	3.58																				19.58										
Quercus virginiana	345	0.96	2.58	0.58				3.92	2.58	12.25		0.25			0.83					0.42	0.17	0.33					0.42	6.83		0.17			
Rhus copallinum	1	0	0.02																						0.08								
Sabal palmetto	2	0.01	0.03								0.08																0.17						
Serenoa repens	23	0.06	0.14			0.17														0.08			0.08	0.42		0.25	0.17		0.58				
Sideroxylon tenax	7	0.02	0.06					0.25					0.08			0.25				0.08													
Smilax laurifolia	1	0	0.02																						0.08								
Symplocos tinctoria	1	0	0.02																											0.08		
Vaccinium arboreum	21	0.06	0.14			0.08									0.25															0.25	0.08	
Vaccinium myrsinites	28	0.08	0.3			1.50						0.58						0.08	0.08	0.67					0.17		0.08						
Vitis rotundifolia	1	0	0.02																											0.00		

Table 6. Percent of vegetation cover (relative cover) and frequency of occurrence of shrub species in vegetation monitoring sampling locations at Cumberland Island National Seashore, 2009.

Species	Frequency	Avg	Std Dev	2	3	4	5	6	7	8	9	11	13	14	15	16	17	18	19	21	22	23	24	26	27	28	29	30	A1	A2	A3	A5	A6
Asimina parviflora	3.33	0.19	1.03						5.65																								
Asimina sp.	3.33	0.07	0.36										1.97																					
Baccharis halimifolia	3.33	0.05	0.28													1.53																		
Cephalanthus occidentalis	3.33	0.15	0.82																														4.52
Decodon verticillatus	3.33	0.65	3.57																														19.58
Diospyros virginiana	3.33	0.03	0.15																														0.82
Gaylussacia frondosa	6.67	0.18	0.7			3.15																			2.26								
Ilex cassine	3.33	0.1	0.55																														3.04
Ilex glabra	6.67	0.26	1.09			5.70																			2.03								
Ilex opaca	16.67	0.86	3.33		0.61			7.75	6.60	17.30		0.43														1.46							
Ilex vomitoria	6.67	1.71	8.04													43.63																		
Juniperus virginiana	3.33	0.06	0.35														1.90																	
Lyonia ferruginea	60	9.99	16.45	0.88	2.24	15.87				50.25	3.35				2.15			52.92	14.04		23.67	3.06		0.24	11.92	8.35	18.69	10.94	14.16	7.57		59.47	
Lyonia fruticosa	3.33	0.03	0.15																						0.83								
Lyonia lucida	10	2.91	9.01																							34.59		29.79		22.90			
Morella cerifera	73.33	13.15	20.29	3.97	15.13	8.65		45.74	10.11	21.42	0.12	32.74	37.14			87.99	18.97			15.72	0.93	1.60	18.67		0.83		1.63	0.59	5.01	0.72	52.59		14.24
Osmanthus americanus	3.33	0.06	0.34						1.88																								
Persea barbonia	50	2.39	6.16	0.15		1.42				0.33	1.98	0.43			0.43			0.37		24.43						1.50	24.16	0.10	2.01	2.25	5.26	6.83	
Pinus elliottii	13.33	0.65	2.87					9.30	2.20			12.94									1.09												
Pinus palustris	3.33	0.13	0.69						3.77																								
Pinus taeda	26.67	7.2	21.25	0.88			36.26					0.43	16.32	100.00	55.15																		
Quercus geminata	6.67	0.33	1.54			1.53																			8.34								
Quercus laurifolia	10	0.93	4.32															2.22					2.07										
Quercus myrtifolia	13.33	0.88	2.97			1.83																			13.47				1.63		1.44		
Quercus virginiana	33.33	3.73	14.63					17.05	3.45						2.50					3.05			79.25			0.08	1.90			0.10	9.54		
Rhus copallinum	3.33	0.04	0.23																							1.25					0.19		
Sabal palmetto	13.33	1.45	6.47													1.31	35.23										5.69				1.17		

Sampling Point

15

Table 6. Continued.

Species	Frequency	Avg	Std Dev	Sampling Point																													
				2	3	4	5	6	7	8	9	11	13	14	15	16	17	18	19	21	22	23	24	26	27	28	29	30	A1	A2	A3	A5	A6
Salix caroliniana	6.67	0.29	1.44													7.86																		0.96
Serenoa repens	76.67	36.05	33.23	62.92	81.42	57.78	55.24	12.40		5.77	94.55	17.35	0.28					25.17	25.88	0.20	43.91	95.34		99.76	45.42	53.73	34.94	54.39	75.56	66.46		22.31	50.68
Sideroxylon tenax	13.33	0.3	1.29					6.98								1.31	0.27		0.44															
Symplocos tinctoria	10	1.24	5.47	2.50																											4.87		
Vaccinium arboreum	60	11.18	17.69	28.70	0.61		4.25		54.96	4.94		48.61	7.71		32.98			19.32	59.65	4.28	30.40						13.00	2.73			19.09	2.73	
Vaccinium corymbosum	10	0.43	1.44																										1.63		5.84		5.34
Vaccinium myrsinites	23.33	1.62	4.96			2.85			3.77						6.80					22.60					14.90							3.19	
Vaccinium stamineum	6.67	0.27	1.39			0.61			7.60																	0.50							
Zanthoxylum clava-hercules	3.33	0.03	0.14					0.78																									

Table 7. Percent area covered (absolute cover) and frequency of occurrence of shrub species sampled in vegetation monitoring sampling locations at Cumberland Island National Seashore, 2009.

Species	Frequency	Avg	Std Dev	Sampling Point																													
				2	3	4	5	6	7	8	9	11	13	14	15	16	17	18	19	21	22	23	24	26	27	28	29	30	A1	A2	A3	A5	A6
Asimina parviflora	3.33	0.06	0.34						1.88																								
Asimina sp.	3.33	0.02	0.13										0.73																			
Baccharis halimifolia	3.33	0.02	0.13													0.73																
Cephalanthus occidentalis	3.33	0.11	0.63																													3.44
Decodon verticillatus	3.33	0.5	2.72																													14.9
Diospyros virginiana	3.33	0.02	0.11																													0.63
Gaylussacia frondosa	6.67	0.17	0.68			3.23																			1.96							
Ilex cassine	3.33	0.08	0.42																													2.31
Ilex glabra	6.67	0.25	1.1			5.83																			1.77							
Ilex opaca	16.67	0.21	0.61		0.21				2.19	2.19		0.21																1.56				
Ilex vomitoria	6.67	0.59	3.06					1.04									16.77															
Juniperus virginiana	3.33	0.02	0.13														0.73															
Lyonia ferruginea	60	4.56	5.77	0.63	0.77	16.25				6.35	2.81				0.63			14.90	3.33		15.83	2.40		0.21	10.42	10.44	7.19	11.67	11.77	7.71		13.6	
Lyonia fruticosa	3.33	0.02	0.13																						0.73							
Lyonia lucida	10	3.28	10.34																							43.25		31.77		23.33		
Morella cerifera	73.33	5.49	9.31	2.81	5.21	8.85		6.15	3.35	2.71	0.1	15.73	13.75			41.98	7.29			8.04	0.63	1.25	0.94		0.73	0.63	0.63	0.63	4.17	0.73	28.13		10.83
Osmanthus americanus	3.33	0.02	0.11						0.63																							
Persea borbonia	50	1.19	2.8	0.10		1.46				0.04	1.67	0.21			0.13			0.10		12.50						1.88	9.29	0.1	1.67	2.29	2.81	1.56	
Pinus elliottii	13.33	0.25	0.9					1.25	0.73				4.79								0.73												
Pinus palustris	3.33	0.04	0.23						1.25																								
Pinus taeda	26.67	1.06	3.18	0.63			5.33					0.21	6.04	1.56	16.06										7.29								
Quercus geminata	6.67	0.3	1.35			1.56																	0.10							0.77	1.25	
Quercus laurifolia	10	0.32	1.6										8.75					0.63														
Quercus myrtifolia	13.33	0.67	2.32			1.88																			11.77				1.35		5.1		
Quercus virginiana	33.33	0.38	0.67				0.63	2.29	1.15						0.73					1.56			3.98			0.10	0.73			0.1	0.1		
Rhus copallinum	3.33	0.05	0.29																							1.56						
Sabal palmetto	13.33	0.57	2.49													0.63	13.54										2.19				0.63		
Salix caroliniana	6.67	0.15	0.69													3.75																0.73
Serenoa repens	76.67	26.27	29.92	44.58	28.02	59.17	8.13	1.67		0.73	79.48	8.33	0.10					7.08	6.15	0.10	29.38	74.58		87.92	39.71	67.19	13.44	58.02	62.81	67.71		5.1	38.56
Sideroxylon tenax	13.33	0.06	0.2					0.94									0.10		0.10					0.63								
Symplocos tinctoria	10	0.65	2.81	1.77																15.21											2.6		
Vaccinium arboreum	60	4.6	7.3	20.33	0.21	0.63	0.63		18.23	0.63		23.35	2.85		9.60			5.44	14.17	2.19	20.33						5.00	2.92			10.21	0.63	0.63
Vaccinium corymbosum	10	0.28	0.94																										1.35		3.13		4.06
Vaccinium myrsinites	23.33	1.07	3.13			2.92			1.25						1.98					11.56					13.02	0.63						0.73	
Vaccinium stamineum	6.67	0.1	0.47			0.63			2.52																							
Zanthoxylum clava-herculis	3.33	0	0.02					0.1																								

Table 8. Percent of vegetation cover (relative cover) and frequency of occurrence of groundcover species in vegetation monitoring sampling locations at Cumberland Island National Seashore, 2009.

Species	Frequency	Avg	Std Dev	Sampling Point																													
				2	3	4	5	6	7	8	9	11	13	14	15	16	17	18	19	21	22	23	24	26	27	28	29	30	A1	A2	A3	A5	A6
Ambrosia artemisiifolia	3.33	0	0.01				0.03																										
Ampelopsis arborea	3.33	0.09	0.48													2.62																	
Andropogon glomeratus	3.33	0.02	0.1														0.53															
Andropogon virginicus	3.33	0.02	0.1														0.53															
Andropogon virginicus var virginicus	20	0.46	1.55		2.95								0.14		0.40			1.04		1.16	8.04											
Aristida sp	3.33	0.05	0.26														1.42															
Aristida stricta	3.33	0.04	0.22					1.19																								
Arundinaria gigantea ssp. gigantea	3.33	0.09	0.5																								2.76					
Axonopus furcatus	16.67	0.18	0.78				4.28		0.20				0.14				0.53				0.16											
Bignonia capreolata	6.67	0.05	0.25							0.25									1.34													
Boehmeria cylindrica	3.33	0.1	0.52													2.87																
Carya glabra	3.33	0	0.01																								0.03					
Cenchrus sp	6.67	0.03	0.13													0.16	0.71															
Centella asiatica	3.33	0	0.03				0.14																									
Chasmanthium laxum	16.67	0.38	1.41															7.60	1.11				0.41				1.44					0.81
Chasmanthium sessiliflorum	16.67	0.11	0.34	1.28	1.38					0.18			0.27								0.16											
Chondroscolus stimulosus	3.33	0	0										0.03																			
Croton punctatus	3.33	0	0														0.02															
Cyperus polystachyos	3.33	0.1	0.55														3.02															
Cyperus sp	33.33	0.3	0.85				3.57	0.20	0.40				0.14				3.20		0.28	0.19	0.32		0.19			0.61						
Decodon verticillatus	3.33	0.01	0.05																												0.30	
Dichanthelium sp	63.33	0.75	0.98		1.38	0.20	1.42	3.18	2.71	0.39		1.16	1.08		0.44		0.80	1.55	1.00	0.08	3.53		0.22		0.58	0.15		1.35		1.42		
Dichondra carolinensis	3.33	0.12	0.66				3.55																									
Diodia teres	10	0.48	1.85				1.70									9.69		3.11														
Distichlis spicata	3.33	0	0.03				0.14																									
Eragrostis sp	3.33	0.01	0.05														0.27															
Erechtites hieracifolius	3.33	0.03	0.15													0.82																
Eremochloa ophiuroides	23.33	1.42	3.94				0.28		1.21				15.31				6.22		15.03		2.37					2.30						
Erigeron quercifolius	3.33	0	0														0.02															
Eupatorium capillifolium	13.33	0.21	0.85				0.28										4.55				0.16				1.26						
Eupatorium sp	3.33	0.08	0.44						2.43																							
Eustachys petraea	3.33	0.06	0.32														1.78															
Euthamia minor	3.33	0.03	0.16				0.85																									
Fimbristylis caroliniana	3.33	0.05	0.29														1.60															
Galactia elliottii	6.67	0.38	1.88			1.18																			10.24						
Galium sp	6.67	0.03	0.15													0.82	0.20															
Gaylussacia frondosa	6.67	0.08	0.31			1.18																			1.26						
Gelsemium sempervirens	20	0.07	0.24				1.30								0.20					0.14		0.19	0.04							0.16		
Helianthemum corymbosum	13.33	0.56	1.82				4.54	0.04									3.91		8.35													

Table 8. Continued.

Species	Frequency	Avg	Std Dev	2	3	4	5	6	7	8	9	11	13	14	15	16	17	18	19	21	22	23	24	26	27	28	29	30	A1	A2	A3	A5	A6
Helianthemum georgianum	3.33	0.04	0.2										1.08																					
Hydrocotyle bonariensis	13.33	0.09	0.26				0.14	0.40								0.96	1.07																	
Hypericum gentianoides	3.33	0.04	0.21														1.16																	
Ilex glabra	3.33	0.01	0.07			0.39																												
Ilex opaca	10	0.01	0.04		0.04							0.23									0.03												
Ilex vomitoria	6.67	0.03	0.13					0.40									0.62																
Ipomoea sp.	3.33	0.01	0.04						0.20																								
Lemna sp	3.33	0.01	0.03																														0.16	
Limnobium spongia	3.33	0.85	4.64																														25.41	
Lyonia ferruginea	43.33	0.19	0.55		1.18					2.86							0.17			0.06	0.21		0.45	0.07	0.21	0.15	0.04		0.24			
Lyonia fruticosa	3.33	0.04	0.2																					1.08								
Lyonia lucida	10	0.2	0.68																						0.71		2.08		3.10			
Melothria pendula	3.33	0.06	0.32													1.77																
Mikania scandens	3.33	0.07	0.37													2.05																
Mimosa microphylla	3.33	0.01	0.04						0.20																								
Morella cerifera	26.67	0.21	0.49		0.20							0.43	2.03			1.12					0.16		1.12									1.13		
Optismenus hirtellus	10	0.53	2.77														0.53						0.19				15.20						
Opuntia humifusa	3.33	0	0														0.02																
Osmunda regalis	3.33	0.05	0.3																															1.62
Panicum hemitomon	6.67	0.56	3.01								0.21			16.52																			
Panicum sp.	20	0.06	0.17		0.08				0.40	0.18			0.14		0.20				0.83	0.19													
Panicum verrucosum	3.33	0.05	0.26											1.40																			
Panicum virgatum	3.33	0.04	0.22					1.19																									
Parietaria sp.	3.33	0	0														0.02																
Parthenocissus quinquefolia	6.67	0.01	0.04					0.20															0.04										
Paspalum notatum	3.33	0.18	0.98														0.80																
Paspalum sp.	10	0.16	0.5				5.39												0.14														
Persea borbonia	40	0.29	0.65									0.19				2.05	1.78	0.17	0.83			1.25			0.21	1.84	0.29		1.10	2.83		
Phyla nodiflora	6.67	0.04	0.2			0.28													0.14													
Physalis viscosa	3.33	0.01	0.04													1.09	0.20																
Pinus taeda	13.33	0.01	0.03		0.04		0.17			0.35																					0.03		
Polygonella gracilis	3.33	0	0.03									0.04							0.14														
Polygonum sp	3.33	0	0.02																															
Polypremum procumbens	3.33	0.03	0.15														0.80																
Prunus serotina	6.67	0	0.01																				0.07			0.03						
Pteridium aquilinum	3.33	0.04	0.23																					1.26								
Quercus geminata	6.67	0.05	0.22			1.18																		0.18								
Quercus laurifolia	26.67	0.23	0.64	0.36		0.20				0.35		0.04	2.63					2.42	0.33	0.39											0.33	
Quercus myrtifolia	6.67	0.08	0.42																								2.31					
Quercus sp.	3.33	0.32	1.74																			9.50										
Quercus virginiana	40	1.02	2.25	1.09				4.17	4.05	9.70		0.08			0.24					1.16	6.18	0.25				0.46	3.05		0.24			
Rhus copallinum	3.33	0	0.01																					0.04								
Rhynchospora latifolia	3.33	0	0.02													0.14																0.14	
Rhynchospora megalocarpa	3.33	0	0.02														0.09																
Rhynchospora sp.	13.33	0.05	0.16		0.20								0.51		0.20								0.19										

Table 8. Continued.

Species	Frequency	Avg	Std Dev	Sampling Point																														
				2	3	4	5	6	7	8	9	11	13	14	15	16	17	18	19	21	22	23	24	26	27	28	29	30	A1	A2	A3	A5	A6
Rubus argutus	10	0.1	0.34				1.70		0.40							0.82																		
Rubus sp.	6.67	0.08	0.43																								0.18					2.36		
Sabal palmetto	3.33	0.01	0.03																															
Saururus cernuus	3.33	0.12	0.67																															3.65
Scleria triglomerata	33.33	1.06	2.95	1.46	0.20			1.19		3.17			9.49		0.60			13.30	0.03				0.04	2.45			2.15				0.16		
Serenoa repens	30	0.28	0.73			1.18					1.25																		2.96				0.04
Sideroxylon tenax	13.33	0.02	0.06					0.20					0.14			0.16			0.14				0.04				0.15						
Smilax auriculata	6.67	0.13	0.67																													0.21	
Smilax bona-nox	20	0.36	0.9					3.89	2.43							2.05	0.98										0.46				1.10		
Smilax glauca	10	0.01	0.03		0.04												0.09																
Smilax laurifolia	6.67	0.01	0.05				0.14									0.27																	
Smilax sp.	30	0.05	0.12			0.08							0.27			0.02		0.03			0.16			0.41	0.04	0.13			0.46				
Spartina bakeri	6.67	1.22	6.45								1.25			35.34																			
Sporobolus virginicus	3.33	0.01	0.05													0.27									0.04								
Stellaria media	13.33	0.05	0.21				1.16												0.09		0.16												
Stillingia sylvatica	3.33	0.01	0.04						0.20																								
Symplocos tinctoria	3.33	0.03	0.17																											0.94		
Vaccinium arboreum	23.33	0.06	0.17			0.04			0.40			0.19						0.17	0.03												0.19		
Vaccinium myrsinites	10	0.14	0.52			1.38														2.52					0.22							
Vitis rotundifolia	53.33	1.83	3.6	6.19			0.85	0.20	8.09	0.04		6.58			0.20	4.64				2.90		0.04	2.98	1.22			0.03		0.12		16.36		4.59

Unidentified

Species	Frequency	Avg	Std Dev	2	3	4	5	6	7	8	9	11	13	14	15	16	17	18	19	21	22	23	24	26	27	28	29	30	A1	A2	A3	A5	A6
Asteraceae	20	0.16	0.76				0.14						0.27	0.00	0.40	0.14	0.16		4.17										0.04				
Cyperaceae	6.67	0.08	0.4													2.18		0.17															
Fabaceae	3.33	0.03	0.18																0.97														
Magnoliopsida	6.67	0.00	0.02										0.03				0.09		0.09														
Poaceae	10	0.26	1.2										0.81				6.58																
Rubiaceae	3.33	0	0.02						0.40								0.09																

Ground Condition

Species	Frequency	Avg	Std Dev	2	3	4	5	6	7	8	9	11	13	14	15	16	17	18	19	21	22	23	24	26	27	28	29	30	A1	A2	A3	A5	A6
Bare ground	73.33	5.9	8.46	15.66	1.18		13.33	0.40	17.39	1.23		0.39	4.36	0.00	0.40	32.07	23.03	2.76	14.75	2.32	14.35		0.56		17.25		5.22		6.35		1.10	2.74	
Exposed humus	3.33	0.12	0.68											3.70																			
Leaf litter or duff	100	73.45	22.28	73.95	91.14	92.27	54.88	83.17	58.66	74.78	97.30	90.63	60.84	43.04	86.18	31.25	26.49	70.64	48.57	88.66	63.23	96.54	84.42	95.47	66.14	95.98	66.80	94.34	85.26	95.32	71.27	95.14	21.08
Open water	6.67	1.63	7.76							6.88					10.89																		42.16
Upland non-vascular plants or lichens	43.33	0.72	2.02			0.20		0.20											0.83			1.71			0.36	2.51		0.20	1.15		0.94	1.54	0.08

20

Table 9. Percent area covered (absolute cover) and frequency of occurrence by groundcover species sampled in vegetation monitoring sampling locations at Cumberland Island National Seashore, 2009.

Species	Frequency	Avg	Std Dev	2	3	4	5	6	7	8	9	11	13	14	15	16	17	18	19	21	22	23	24	26	27	28	29	30	A1	A2	A3	A5	A6
Ambrosia artemisiifolia	3.33	0	0.01				0.04																											
Ampelopsis arborea	3.33	0.13	0.73																															
Andropogon glomeratus	3.33	0.04	0.23														1.25																
Andropogon virginicus	3.33	0.04	0.23														1.25																
Andropogon virginicus var. virginicus	20	0.56	2		3.13								0.21		0.42			1.25		1.25	10.63											
Aristida sp.	3.33	0.11	0.61																														
Aristida stricta	3.33	0.04	0.23														3.33																
Arundinaria gigantea ssp. gigantea	3.33	0.13	0.88					1.25																				3.75					
Axonopus furcatus	16.67	0.27	1.16				6.29		0.21				0.21				1.25				0.21												
Bignonia capreolata	6.67	0.06	0.37							0.29									2														
Boehmeria cylindrica	3.33	0.15	0.6													4.38																	
Carex glabra	3.33	0	0.01																									0.04					
Cenchrus sp.	6.67	0.06	0.31													0.25	1.67																
Centella asiatica	3.33	0.01	0.04				0.21																										
Chasmanthium laxum	16.67	0.48	1.72															9.17	1.67				0.46				1.96					
Chasmanthium sessiliflorum	16.67	0.13	0.37	1.46	1.46					0.21											0.21											1.25
Cnidoscolus stimulosus	3.33	0	0.01										0.04																				
Croton punctatus	3.33	0	0.01														0.04																
Cyperus polystachyos	3.33	0.24	1.29														7.08																
Cyperus sp.	33.33	0.52	1.63				5.25	0.21	0.42				0.21				7.5		0.42	0.21	0.42		0.21			0.83						
Decodon verticillatus	3.33	0.02	0.08																														0.46
Dichanthelium sp.	63.33	0.94	1.19		1.46	0.21	2.08	3.33	2.79	0.46		1.25	1.67		0.46	1.88	1.88	1.5		0.08	4.67		0.25		0.67		0.21	1.46		1.88		
Dichondra carolinensis	3.33	0.17	0.95				5.21																										
Diodia teres	10	0.32	2.95													14.79									7.29								
Distichlis spicata	3.33	0.01	0.04				0.21																										
Eragrostis sp.	3.33	0.02	0.11														0.63																
Erechtites hieraciifolius	3.33	0.04	0.23													1.25																	
Eremochloa ophiuroides	23.33	2.26	6.26						1.25				23.54				14.58		2.25		3.13					3.13						
Erigeron quercifolius	3.33	0	0.01														0.04																
Eupatorium capillifolium	13.33	0.43	1.95				0.42										10.67								1.46							
Eupatorium sp.	3.33	0.08	0.46						2.5																								
Eustachys petraea	3.33	0.14	0.76														4.17																
Euthamia minor	3.33	0.04	0.23				1.25																										
Fimbristylis caroliniana	3.33	0.13	0.68														3.75																
Galactia elliottii	6.67	0.44	2.17			1.25																		11.88								
Galium sp.	6.67	0.06	0.24													1.25	0.46																
Gaylussacia frondosa	6.67	0.09	0.34			1.25																		1.46								
Gelsemium sempervirens	20	0.09	0.35				1.92								0.21				0.21	0.21			0.04							0.21		
Helianthemum corymbosum	13.33	0.95	2.96				6.67	0.04								9.17			12.5													
Helianthemum georgianum	3.33	0.06	0.3										1.67																				
Hydrocotyle bonariensis	13.33	0.15	0.52				0.21	0.42								1.46	2.5																

Table 9. Continued.

Species	Frequency	Avg	Std Dev	2	3	4	5	6	7	8	9	11	13	14	15	16	17	18	19	21	22	23	24	26	27	28	29	30	A1	A2	A3	A5	A6
Hypericum gentianoides	3.33	0.09	0.49						2.71																									
Ilex glabra	3.33	0.01	0.08																															
Ilex opaca	10	0.01	0.05	0.25																	0.04		0.42										
Ilex vomitoria	6.67	0.06	0.27														1.46																
Ipomoea sp.	3.33	0.01	0.04					0.42	0.21					0.04																				0.25
Lemna sp.	3.33	0.01	0.05																															39.17
Limnobium spongia	3.33	1.31	7.15							3.38																								
Lyonia ferruginea	43.33	0.22	0.64		1.25	0.04						0.04						0.21			0.08	0.21		0.46	0.08	0.21	0.21	0.04			0.25		
Lyonia fruticosa	3.33	0.04	0.23																						1.25								
Lyonia lucida	10	0.2	0.66																							0.71		2.13			3.17		
Melothria pendula	3.33	0.09	0.49													2.71																	
Mikania scandens	3.33	0.1	0.57													3.13																	
Mimosa microphylla	3.33	0.01	0.04						0.21																								
Morella cerifera	26.67	0.29	0.7		0.21							0.46	3.13			1.71	1.25				0.21		1.25									1.5		
Oplismenus hirtellus	10	0.74	3.76														1.25											20.63					
Opuntia humilusa	3.33	0	0.01														0.04																
Osmunda regalis	3.33	0.08	0.46																				0.21										2.5
Panicum hemitomon	6.67	1.15	6.27								0.21			34.38																			
Panicum sp.	20	0.06	0.24						0.42	0.21			0.21		0.21				1.25	0.21														
Panicum verrucosum	3.33	0.1	0.53											2.92																			
Panicum virgatum	3.33	0.04	0.23					1.25																									
Parietaria sp.	3.33	0	0.01																															
Parthenocissus quinquefolia	6.67	0.01	0.04					0.21									0.04						0.04										
Paspalum notatum	3.33	0.26	1.45				7.92																											
Paspalum sp.	10	0.28	0.95													3.13	4.17	0.21	1.25						1.46								
Persea borbonia	40	0.34	0.83		0.08	0.29						0.21				1.67	0.04	0.21	0.21	0.21		1.25			0.21	2.5	0.29		1.13	3.75		
Phyla nodiflora	6.67	0.06	0.3														0.46																
Physalis viscosa	3.33	0.02	0.08				0.25																										
Pinus taeda	13.33	0.01	0.05		0.04							0.04																		0.04		
Polygonella gracilis	3.33	0.01	0.04																0.21														
Polygonum sp.	3.33	0.01	0.04																														0.21
Polypremum procumbens	3.33	0.06	0.34														1.88																
Prunus serotina	6.67	0	0.02																				0.08				0.04					
Pteridium aquilinum	3.33	0.05	0.27																						1.46							
Quercus geminata	6.67	0.05	0.23		0.21																				0.21							
Quercus laurifolia	26.67	0.3	0.89	0.42						0.42								2.92	0.5	0.42								2.5		0.33	
Quercus myrtifolia	6.67	0.09	0.46		0.21	0.21								4.04																		
Quercus sp.	3.33	0.35	1.94															10.63														
Quercus virginiana	40	1.18	2.67	1.25				4.38	4.17	11.46		0.08	14.58		0.25					1.25	8.17	0.25				0.63	3.13		0.25		
Rhus copallinum	3.33	0.01	0.01																							0.04						
Rhynchospora latifolia	3.33	0.01	0.04													0.21																
Rhynchospora megalocarpa	3.33	0.01	0.04														0.21																
Rhynchospora sp.	13.33	0.06	0.23		0.21								1.25		0.21								0.21										
Rubus sp.	10	0.14	0.51				2.5									1.25									1.46		0.25			3.13		
Rubus argutus	6.67	0.11	0.57						0.42														0.04									
Sabal palmetto	3.33	0.01	0.05																									2.5				
Saururus cernuus	3.33	0.1	1.03															16.04	0.04													5.63
Scleria triglomerata	33.33	1.38	3.9	1.67	0.21			1.25		3.75			14.58		0.63									2.5		2.92						
Serenoa repens	90	0.29	0.77		0.21	1.25					1.25		0.21							0.04			0.04			0.25	0.21		3.21		0.21		0.04
Sideroxylon tenax	13.33	0.03	0.08		0.21			0.21					0.21			0.25			0.21														0.04

Table 9. Continued.

Species	Frequency	Avg	Std Dev	2	3	4	5	6	7	8	9	11	13	14	15	16	17	18	19	21	22	23	24	26	27	28	29	30	A1	A2	A3	A5	A6
Smilax auriculata	6.67	0.29	1.56														8.54															0.21	
Smilax bona-nox	20	0.47	1.08					4.08	2.5							3.13	2.29										0.63					1.46		
Smilax glauca	10	0.02	0.05		0.04												0.21																
Smilax laurifolia	6.67	0.02	0.08													0.42									0.04								
Smilax sp.	30	0.06	0.14			0.08							0.42				0.04		0.04					0.42	0.04	0.13				0.5				
Spartina bakeri	6.67	2.49	13.42								1.25			73.54																				
Sporobolus virginicus	3.33	0.01	0.06													0.42																	
Stellaria media	13.33	0.08	0.31				1.71										0.21																
Stillingia sylvatica	3.33	0.01	0.04						0.21																								
Symplocos tinctoria	3.33	0.04	0.23																													1.25		
Vaccinium arboreum	23.33	0.08	0.24			0.04			0.42			0.21			0.04			0.21														0.25		
Vaccinium myrsinites	10	0.15	0.55			1.46													1.25	2.71					0.25								
Vitis rotundifolia	53.33	2.27	4.59	7.08			1.25	0.21	8.33	0.04		7.08			0.21	7.08			3.13			0.04	3.33	1.25			0.04		0.13		21.67		7.08
Unidentified																																
Asteraceae	20	0.25	1.14				0.21						0.42			0.21	0.42		6.25											0.04				
Cyperaceae	6.67	0.12	0.61													3.33		0.21															
Fabaceae	3.33	0.05	0.27																1.46														
Magnoliopsida	6.67	0.01	0.04										0.04				0.21																
Poaceae	10	0.57	2.81						0.42								15.42																
Rubiaceae	3.33	0.01	0.04														0.21																
Ground Condition																																
Bare ground	73.33	8.49	13.89	17.92	1.25		19.58	0.42	17.92	1.46		0.42	6.71	0	0.42	48.96	53.96	3.33	22.08	2.5	18.96		0.63		20		7.08		0.04		1.46	2.75	
Exposed humus	3.33	0.26	1.41											7.71																			
Leaf litter or duff	100	85.63	15.97	84.58	96.46	97.5	80.63	87.29	60.42	88.33	97.5	97.5	93.54	89.58	89.38	47.71	62.08	85.21	72.71	95.42	83.54	96.46	94.38	97.5	76.67	95.42	90.63	98.46	92.29	97.5	94.38	95.42	32.5
Open water	6.67	2.44	11.91							8.13					11.29																		65
Upland non-vascular plants or lichens	43.33	0.77	2.1	0.21		0.21		0.21	0.21			0.21	1.25						1.25			1.71			0.42	2.5	0.21		1.25		1.25	1.54	0.13

Literature Cited

Bechtold, W. A. and P. L. Patterson, (eds.). 2005. The enhanced forest inventory and analysis program — national sampling design and estimation procedures. General Technical Report SRS-80. USDA Forest Service, Southern Research Station, Asheville, NC. 85 pp.

DeVivo, J. C., C. J. Wright, M. W. Byrne, E. DiDonato, and T. Curtis. 2008. Vital signs monitoring in the Southeast Coast Inventory & Monitoring Network. Natural Resource Report NPS/SECN/NRR—2008/061. USDI National Park Service, Fort Collins, CO, USA.

Federal Geographic Data Committee. 2008. National vegetation classification standard, version 2. FGDC-STD-005-2008. Available online: http://www.fgdc.gov/standards/project/FGDC-standards-projects/vegetation.

Foster, D. R., G. Motzkin, and B. Slater. 1998. Land-use history as long-term broad-scale disturbance: regional forest dynamics in central New England. Ecosystems: 1:96-119.

Fraedrich S. W., T. C. Harrington, R. J. Rabaglia, M. D. Ulyshen, A. E. Mayfield III, J. L. Hanula, J. M. Eickwort, and D. R. Miller. 2008. A fungal symbiont of the redbay ambrosia beetle causes a lethal wilt in redbay and other Lauraceae in the southeastern United States. Plant Disease 92:215–224.

Haack, R. A. 2006. Exotic bark- and wood-boring Coleoptera in the United States: Recent establishments and interceptions. Canadian Journal of Forest Research 36:269-288.

NPSpecies - The National Park Service Biodiversity Database. Secure online version. https://science1.nature.nps.gov/npspecies/web/main/start (Park list: accessed 1/13/2011).

Peet R. K., T. R. Wentworth, and P. S White. 1998. A flexible, multipurpose method for recording vegetation composition and structure. Castanea 63:262-274.

Rabaglia, R. 2003. Xyleborus glabratus. Online record, URL: http://spfnic.fs.fed.us/exfor/data/pestreports.cfm?pestidval=148&langdisplay=english (Accessed 2/14/2012).

Theobald, D. M., D. L. Stevens, D. White, N. S. Urquhart, A. R. Olsen, and J. B. Norman. 2007. Using GIS to generate spatially balanced random survey designs for natural resource applications Environmental Management 40:134-146.

Turner, II, B. L., W. C. Clark, R. W. Kates, J. F. Richards, J. T. Mathews, and W. B. Meyer, (eds.). 1990. The earth as transformed by human action: Global and regional changes in the biosphere over the past 300 years. Cambridge University Press, Cambridge, UK.

Appendix A. Plant species known to occur at Cumberland Island National Seashore.

Table A-1. Vascular plant species known occur at Cumberland Island National Seashore (NPSpecies 2011), and species detected during 2009 monitoring efforts.

Family	Species	NPSpecies	This study
Acanthaceae	*Dyschoriste oblongifolia*	X	
Acanthaceae	*Ruellia caroliniensis*	X	
Aceraceae	*Acer rubrum*	X	
Agavaceae	*Yucca aloifolia*	X	
Agavaceae	*Yucca filamentosa*	X	
Agavaceae	*Yucca gloriosa*	X	
Aizoaceae	*Sesuvium maritimum*	X	
Aizoaceae	*Sesuvium portulacastrum*	X	
Alismataceae	*Sagittaria graminea*	X	
Alismataceae	*Sagittaria lancifolia*	X	
Alismataceae	*Sagittaria latifolia*	X	
Alismataceae	*Sagittaria subulata var. subulata*	X	
Amaranthaceae	*Alternanthera philoxeroides*	X	
Amaranthaceae	*Amaranthus blitum*	X	
Amaranthaceae	*Froelichia floridana*	X	
Anacardiaceae	*Rhus copallinum*	X	X
Anacardiaceae	*Rhus radicans*	X	
Anacardiaceae	*Toxicodendron radicans*	X	
Annonaceae	*Asimina angustifolia*	X	
Annonaceae	*Asimina incana*	X	
Annonaceae	*Asimina parviflora*	X	X
Annonaceae	*Asimina pygmea*	X	
Annonaceae	*Asimina triloba*	X	
Apiaceae	*Centella asiatica*	X	X
Apiaceae	*Cyclospermum leptophyllum*	X	
Apiaceae	*Hydrocotyle bonariensis*	X	X
Apiaceae	*Hydrocotyle ranunculoides*	X	
Apiaceae	*Hydrocotyle umbellata*	X	
Apiaceae	*Hydrocotyle verticillata*	X	
Apiaceae	*Hydrocotyle verticillata var. triradiata*	X	
Apiaceae	*Ptilimnium capillaceum*	X	
Apiaceae	*Sanicula canadensis*	X	
Apocynaceae	*Nerium oleander*	X	
Apocynaceae	*Trachelospermum jasminoides*	X	
Aquifoliaceae	*Ilex ambigua*	X	
Aquifoliaceae	*Ilex cassine*	X	X
Aquifoliaceae	*Ilex cassine var. cassine*	X	
Aquifoliaceae	*Ilex glabra*	X	X
Aquifoliaceae	*Ilex opaca*	X	X

Table A-1. Continued.

Family	Species	NPSpecies	This study
Aquifoliaceae	*Ilex opaca var. opaca*	X	
Aquifoliaceae	*Ilex vomitoria*	X	X
Araceae	*Arisaema triphyllum*	X	
Araceae	*Colocasia esculenta*	X	
Araceae	*Peltandra sagittifolia*	X	
Araliaceae	*Aralia spinosa*	X	
Araliaceae	*Hedera helix*	X	
Arecaceae	*Phoenix dactylifera*	X	
Arecaceae	*Sabal palmetto*	X	X
Arecaceae	*Serenoa repens*	X	X
Aristolochiaceae	*Aristolochia serpentaria*	X	
Asclepiadaceae	*Asclepias humistrata*	X	
Asclepiadaceae	*Asclepias longifolia*	X	
Asclepiadaceae	*Asclepias verticillata*	X	
Asclepiadaceae	*Cynanchum angustifolium*	X	
Asclepiadaceae	*Cynanchum scoparium*	X	
Asclepiadaceae	*Matelea gonocarpos*	X	
Aspleniaceae	*Asplenium platyneuron*	X	
Asteraceae	*Ageratina jucunda*	X	
Asteraceae	*Ambrosia artemisiifolia*	X	X
Asteraceae	*Aster dumosus*	X	
Asteraceae	*Aster subulatus var. ligulatus*	X	
Asteraceae	*Baccharis angustifolia*	X	
Asteraceae	*Baccharis halimifolia*	X	X
Asteraceae	*Bidens alba var. radiata*	X	
Asteraceae	*Bidens bipinnata*	X	
Asteraceae	*Bidens laevis*	X	
Asteraceae	*Borrichia frutescens*	X	
Asteraceae	*Carduus smallii*	X	
Asteraceae	*Carduus spinosissimus*	X	
Asteraceae	*Carphephorus odoratissimus*	X	
Asteraceae	*Chrysopsis graminifolia*	X	
Asteraceae	*Chrysopsis mariana*	X	
Asteraceae	*Cirsium horridulum*	X	
Asteraceae	*Cirsium nuttallii*	X	
Asteraceae	*Cirsium repandum*	X	
Asteraceae	*Cirsium virginianum*	X	
Asteraceae	*Conyza canadensis var. canadensis*	X	
Asteraceae	*Conyza canadensis var. pusilla*	X	
Asteraceae	*Eclipta prostrata*	X	
Asteraceae	*Elephantopus elatus*	X	
Asteraceae	*Elephantopus nudatus*	X	
Asteraceae	*Elephantopus tomentosus*	X	

Table A-1. Continued.

Family	Species	NPSpecies	This study
Asteraceae	*Erechtites hieraciifolius*	X	X
Asteraceae	*Erigeron canadensis*	X	
Asteraceae	*Erigeron quercifolius*	X	X
Asteraceae	*Erigeron vernus*	X	
Asteraceae	*Eupatorium album*	X	
Asteraceae	*Eupatorium aromaticum*	X	
Asteraceae	*Eupatorium capillifolium*	X	X
Asteraceae	*Eupatorium compositifolium*	X	
Asteraceae	*Eupatorium leptophyllum*	X	
Asteraceae	*Eupatorium mohrii*	X	
Asteraceae	*Eupatorium rugosum*	X	
Asteraceae	*Eupatorium serotinum*	X	
Asteraceae	*Euthamia caroliniana*	X	
Asteraceae	*Euthamia minor*	X	X
Asteraceae	*Euthamia tenuifolia*	X	
Asteraceae	*Gaillardia aestivalis*	X	
Asteraceae	*Gaillardia pulchella*	X	
Asteraceae	*Gamochaeta falcata*	X	
Asteraceae	*Gamochaeta pensylvanica*	X	
Asteraceae	*Gamochaeta purpurea*	X	
Asteraceae	*Gnaphalium obtusifolium*	X	
Asteraceae	*Helenium amarum*	X	
Asteraceae	*Helianthus argophyllus*	X	
Asteraceae	*Heterotheca graminifolia*	X	
Asteraceae	*Heterotheca subaxillaris*	X	
Asteraceae	*Hieracium gronovii*	X	
Asteraceae	*Iva frutescens*	X	
Asteraceae	*Iva imbricata*	X	
Asteraceae	*Krigia virginica*	X	
Asteraceae	*Lactuca graminifolia*	X	
Asteraceae	*Liatris gracilis*	X	
Asteraceae	*Liatris spicata*	X	
Asteraceae	*Liatris tenuifolia var. quadriflora*	X	
Asteraceae	*Liatris tenuifolia var. tenuifolia*	X	
Asteraceae	*Mikania scandens*	X	X
Asteraceae	*Oclemena reticulata*	X	
Asteraceae	*Pityopsis adenolepis*	X	
Asteraceae	*Pityopsis graminifolia*	X	
Asteraceae	*Pityopsis graminifolia var. tenuifolia*	X	
Asteraceae	*Pityopsis pinifolia*	X	
Asteraceae	*Pluchea foetida*	X	
Asteraceae	*Pluchea odorata*	X	
Asteraceae	*Pluchea purpurascens*	X	

Table A-1. Continued.

Family	Species	NPSpecies	This study
Asteraceae	*Pluchea rosea*	X	
Asteraceae	*Pterocaulon virgatum*	X	
Asteraceae	*Pyrrhopappus carolinianus*	X	
Asteraceae	*Senecio vulgaris*	X	
Asteraceae	*Solidago odora*	X	
Asteraceae	*Solidago odora var. chapmanii*	X	
Asteraceae	*Solidago sempervirens*	X	
Asteraceae	*Solidago tenuifolia*	X	
Asteraceae	*Solidago tortifolia*	X	
Asteraceae	*Sonchus asper*	X	
Asteraceae	*Sonchus oleraceus*	X	
Asteraceae	*Symphyotrichum subulatum*	X	
Asteraceae	*Symphyotrichum tenuifolium*	X	
Asteraceae	*Verbesina occidentalis*	X	
Asteraceae	*Youngia japonica*	X	
Azollaceae	*Azolla caroliniana*	X	
Bataceae	*Batis maritima*	X	
Bignoniaceae	*Bignonia capreolata*	X	X
Bignoniaceae	*Campsis radicans*	X	
Blechnaceae	*Woodwardia areolata*	X	
Blechnaceae	*Woodwardia virginica*	X	
Boraginaceae	*Heliotropium curassavicum*	X	
Brassicaceae	*Barbarea vulgaris*	X	
Brassicaceae	*Cakile edentula ssp. harperi*	X	
Brassicaceae	*Cakile harperi*	X	
Brassicaceae	*Cardamine pensylvanica*	X	
Brassicaceae	*Descurainia pinnata*	X	
Brassicaceae	*Lepidium virginicum*	X	
Bromeliaceae	*Tillandsia recurvata*	X	
Bromeliaceae	*Tillandsia setacea*	X	
Bromeliaceae	*Tillandsia usneoides*	X	
Buddlejaceae	*Polypremum procumbens*	X	X
Burmanniaceae	*Burmannia biflora*	X	
Cabombaceae	*Brasenia schreberi*	X	
Cabombaceae	*Cabomba caroliniana*	X	
Cactaceae	*Opuntia ficus-indica*	X	
Cactaceae	*Opuntia humifusa*	X	X
Cactaceae	*Opuntia pusilla*	X	
Campanulaceae	*Specularia perfoliata*	X	
Campanulaceae	*Triodanis perfoliata*	X	
Campanulaceae	*Wahlenbergia marginata*	X	
Caprifoliaceae	*Lonicera japonica*	X	
Caprifoliaceae	*Lonicera sempervirens*	X	

Table A-1. Continued.

Family	Species	NPSpecies	This study
Caprifoliaceae	*Sambucus canadensis*	X	
Caprifoliaceae	*Sambucus nigra ssp. canadensis*	X	
Caprifoliaceae	*Sambucus simpsonii*	X	
Caryophyllaceae	*Arenaria serpyllifolia*	X	
Caryophyllaceae	*Arenaria serpyllifolia ssp. serpyllifolia*	X	
Caryophyllaceae	*Cerastium glomeratum*	X	
Caryophyllaceae	*Paronychia riparia*	X	
Caryophyllaceae	*Polycarpon tetraphyllum*	X	
Caryophyllaceae	*Sagina decumbens*	X	
Caryophyllaceae	*Scleranthus annuus*	X	
Caryophyllaceae	*Silene antirrhina*	X	
Caryophyllaceae	*Spergularia salina*	X	
Caryophyllaceae	*Stellaria media*	X	X
Ceratophyllaceae	*Ceratophyllum demersum*	X	
Ceratophyllaceae	*Ceratophyllum echinatum*	X	
Chenopodiaceae	*Atriplex cristata*	X	
Chenopodiaceae	*Chenopodium album*	X	
Chenopodiaceae	*Chenopodium ambrosioides*	X	
Chenopodiaceae	*Salicornia bigelovii*	X	
Chenopodiaceae	*Salicornia maritima*	X	
Chenopodiaceae	*Salicornia virginica*	X	
Chenopodiaceae	*Salsola kali*	X	
Chenopodiaceae	*Sarcocornia perennis*	X	
Chenopodiaceae	*Suaeda linearis*	X	
Cistaceae	*Helianthemum canadense*	X	
Cistaceae	*Helianthemum carolinianum*	X	
Cistaceae	*Helianthemum corymbosum*	X	X
Cistaceae	*Helianthemum georgianum*	X	X
Cistaceae	*Lechea leggettii*	X	
Cistaceae	*Lechea mucronata*	X	
Clusiaceae	*Hypericum cistifolium*	X	
Clusiaceae	*Hypericum crux-andreae*	X	
Clusiaceae	*Hypericum fasciculatum*	X	
Clusiaceae	*Hypericum gentianoides*	X	X
Clusiaceae	*Hypericum hypericoides*	X	
Clusiaceae	*Hypericum mutilum*	X	
Clusiaceae	*Hypericum myrtifolium*	X	
Commelinaceae	*Commelina erecta*	X	
Commelinaceae	*Commelina virginica*	X	
Commelinaceae	*Tradescantia ohiensis*	X	
Convolvulaceae	*Calystegia sepium*	X	
Convolvulaceae	*Dichondra carolinensis*	X	X
Convolvulaceae	*Ipomoea cordatotriloba*	X	

Table A-1. Continued.

Family	Species	NPSpecies	This study
Convolvulaceae	*Ipomoea imperati*	X	
Convolvulaceae	*Ipomoea pes-caprae*	X	
Convolvulaceae	*Ipomoea quamoclit*	X	
Convolvulaceae	*Ipomoea sagittata*	X	
Convolvulaceae	*Stylisma patens*	X	
Cornaceae	*Cornus florida*	X	
Cornaceae	*Cornus foemina*	X	
Cornaceae	*Cornus foemina*	X	
Cucurbitaceae	*Melothria pendula*	X	X
Cupressaceae	*Cupressus sempervirens*	X	
Cupressaceae	*Juniperus silicicola*	X	
Cupressaceae	*Juniperus virginiana*	X	X
Cuscutaceae	*Cuscuta pentagona*	X	
Cuscutaceae	*Cuscuta rostrata*	X	
Cycadaceae	*Cycas revoluta*	X	
Cyperaceae	*Bolboschoenus robustus*	X	
Cyperaceae	*Bulbostylis barbata*	X	
Cyperaceae	*Bulbostylis ciliatifolia*	X	
Cyperaceae	*Bulbostylis ciliatifolia var. ciliatifolia*	X	
Cyperaceae	*Bulbostylis stenophylla*	X	
Cyperaceae	*Carex albolutescens*	X	
Cyperaceae	*Carex bromoides*	X	
Cyperaceae	*Carex dasycarpa*	X	
Cyperaceae	*Carex festucacea*	X	
Cyperaceae	*Carex fissa var. aristata*	X	
Cyperaceae	*Carex howei*	X	
Cyperaceae	*Carex joorii*	X	
Cyperaceae	*Carex lupulina*	X	
Cyperaceae	*Carex lurida*	X	
Cyperaceae	*Carex muehlenbergii*	X	
Cyperaceae	*Carex normalis*	X	
Cyperaceae	*Carex stipata*	X	
Cyperaceae	*Carex verrucosa*	X	
Cyperaceae	*Cladium jamaicense*	X	
Cyperaceae	*Cyperus croceus*	X	
Cyperaceae	*Cyperus distinctus*	X	
Cyperaceae	*Cyperus erythrorhizos*	X	
Cyperaceae	*Cyperus esculentus*	X	
Cyperaceae	*Cyperus esculentus*	X	
Cyperaceae	*Cyperus filicinus*	X	
Cyperaceae	*Cyperus filiculmis*	X	
Cyperaceae	*Cyperus haspan*	X	
Cyperaceae	*Cyperus odoratus*	X	

Table A-1. Continued.

Family	Species	NPSpecies	This study
Cyperaceae	*Cyperus plukenetii*	X	
Cyperaceae	*Cyperus polystachyos*	X	X
Cyperaceae	*Cyperus polystachyos var. filicinus*	X	
Cyperaceae	*Cyperus polystachyos var. texensis*	X	
Cyperaceae	*Cyperus pseudovegetus*	X	
Cyperaceae	*Cyperus retrorsus*	X	
Cyperaceae	*Cyperus rotundus*	X	
Cyperaceae	*Cyperus surinamensis*	X	
Cyperaceae	*Cyperus virens*	X	
Cyperaceae	*Dulichium arundinaceum*	X	
Cyperaceae	*Eleocharis albida*	X	
Cyperaceae	*Eleocharis equisetoides*	X	
Cyperaceae	*Eleocharis fallax*	X	
Cyperaceae	*Eleocharis flavescens*	X	
Cyperaceae	*Eleocharis montevidensis*	X	
Cyperaceae	*Eleocharis robbinsii*	X	
Cyperaceae	*Eleocharis vivipara*	X	
Cyperaceae	*Fimbristylis autumnalis*	X	
Cyperaceae	*Fimbristylis caroliniana*	X	X
Cyperaceae	*Fimbristylis castanea*	X	
Cyperaceae	*Fimbristylis puberula*	X	
Cyperaceae	*Fimbristylis thermalis*	X	
Cyperaceae	*Fuirena pumila*	X	
Cyperaceae	*Fuirena squarrosa*	X	
Cyperaceae	*Kyllinga brevifolia*	X	
Cyperaceae	*Kyllinga pumila*	X	
Cyperaceae	*Lipocarpha micrantha*	X	
Cyperaceae	*Rhynchospora colorata*	X	
Cyperaceae	*Rhynchospora corniculata*	X	
Cyperaceae	*Rhynchospora decurrens*	X	
Cyperaceae	*Rhynchospora fascicularis*	X	
Cyperaceae	*Rhynchospora inexpansa*	X	
Cyperaceae	*Rhynchospora latifolia*		X
Cyperaceae	*Rhynchospora megalocarpa*		X
Cyperaceae	*Rhynchospora microcephala*	X	
Cyperaceae	*Rhynchospora miliacea*	X	
Cyperaceae	*Rhynchospora scirpoides*	X	
Cyperaceae	*Rhynchospora wrightiana*	X	
Cyperaceae	*Schoenoplectus americanus*	X	
Cyperaceae	*Schoenoplectus tabernaemontani*	X	
Cyperaceae	*Scirpus cyperinus*	X	
Cyperaceae	*Scirpus pungens*	X	
Cyperaceae	*Scleria oligantha*	X	

Family	Species	NPSpecies	This study
Cyperaceae	*Scleria triglomerata*	X	X
Cyperaceae	*Websteria confervoides*	X	
Dennstaedtiaceae	*Pteridium aquilinum*	X	X
Dennstaedtiaceae	*Pteridium aquilinum var. latiusculum*	X	
Droseraceae	*Drosera rotundifolia*	X	
Ebenaceae	*Diospyros virginiana*	X	X
Ericaceae	*Befaria racemosa*	X	
Ericaceae	*Gaylussacia frondosa*	X	X
Ericaceae	*Gaylussacia frondosa var. tomentosa*	X	
Ericaceae	*Kalmia hirsuta*	X	
Ericaceae	*Leucothoe racemosa*	X	
Ericaceae	*Lyonia ferruginea*	X	X
Ericaceae	*Lyonia fruticosa*		X
Ericaceae	*Lyonia lucida*	X	X
Ericaceae	*Lyonia mariana*	X	
Ericaceae	*Vaccinium arboreum*	X	X
Ericaceae	*Vaccinium corymbosum*	X	X
Ericaceae	*Vaccinium fuscatum*	X	
Ericaceae	*Vaccinium myrsinites*	X	X
Ericaceae	*Vaccinium stamineum*	X	X
Ericaceae	*Vaccinium stamineum var. stamineum*	X	
Euphorbiaceae	*Acalypha gracilens*	X	
Euphorbiaceae	*Acalypha ostryifolia*	X	
Euphorbiaceae	*Chamaesyce bombensis*	X	
Euphorbiaceae	*Chamaesyce hirta*	X	
Euphorbiaceae	*Chamaesyce hypericifolia*	X	
Euphorbiaceae	*Chamaesyce hyssopifolia*	X	
Euphorbiaceae	*Chamaesyce maculata*	X	
Euphorbiaceae	*Chamaesyce polygonifolia*	X	
Euphorbiaceae	*Chamaesyce prostrata*	X	
Euphorbiaceae	*Cnidoscolus stimulosus*	X	X
Euphorbiaceae	*Croton glandulosus*	X	
Euphorbiaceae	*Croton glandulosus var. glandulosus*	X	
Euphorbiaceae	*Croton punctatus*	X	X
Euphorbiaceae	*Euphorbia cyathophora*	X	
Euphorbiaceae	*Euphorbia heterophylla*	X	
Euphorbiaceae	*Euphorbia heterophylla var. graminifolia*	X	
Euphorbiaceae	*Phyllanthus abnormis*	X	
Euphorbiaceae	*Phyllanthus caroliniensis*	X	
Euphorbiaceae	*Phyllanthus tenellus*	X	
Euphorbiaceae	*Poinsettia cyathophora*	X	
Euphorbiaceae	*Ricinus communis*	X	
Euphorbiaceae	*Stillingia sylvatica*	X	X
Euphorbiaceae	*Tragia urens*	X	
Euphorbiaceae	*Vernicia fordii*	X	

Table A-1. Continued.

Family	Species	NPSpecies	This study
Fabaceae	*Acacia farnesiana*	X	
Fabaceae	*Aeschynomene viscidula*	X	
Fabaceae	*Albizia julibrissin*	X	
Fabaceae	*Amorpha fruticosa*	X	
Fabaceae	*Astragalus villosus*	X	
Fabaceae	*Cassia fasciculata*	X	
Fabaceae	*Cassia nictitans*	X	
Fabaceae	*Centrosema virginianum*	X	
Fabaceae	*Cercis canadensis*	X	
Fabaceae	*Chamaecrista nictitans var. nictitans*	X	
Fabaceae	*Clitoria mariana*	X	
Fabaceae	*Crotalaria mucronata*	X	
Fabaceae	*Crotalaria pallida*	X	
Fabaceae	*Crotalaria pallida var. obovata*	X	
Fabaceae	*Crotalaria purshii*	X	
Fabaceae	*Crotalaria rotundifolia*	X	
Fabaceae	*Crotalaria sagittalis*	X	
Fabaceae	*Crotalaria spectabilis*	X	
Fabaceae	*Desmodium incanum*	X	
Fabaceae	*Desmodium lineatum*	X	
Fabaceae	*Erythrina herbacea*	X	
Fabaceae	*Galactia elliottii*	X	X
Fabaceae	*Galactia regularis*	X	
Fabaceae	*Galactia volubilis*	X	
Fabaceae	*Indigofera caroliniana*	X	
Fabaceae	*Lespedeza hirta*	X	
Fabaceae	*Lupinus villosus*	X	
Fabaceae	*Medicago lupulina*	X	
Fabaceae	*Medicago minima*	X	
Fabaceae	*Medicago polymorpha*	X	
Fabaceae	*Mimosa microphylla*	X	X
Fabaceae	*Mimosa quadrivalvis var. angustata*	X	
Fabaceae	*Rhynchosia difformis*	X	
Fabaceae	*Senna obtusifolia*	X	
Fabaceae	*Senna occidentalis*	X	
Fabaceae	*Sesbania herbacea*	X	
Fabaceae	*Sesbania punicea*	X	
Fabaceae	*Strophostyles helvola*	X	
Fabaceae	*Strophostyles umbellata*	X	
Fabaceae	*Stylosanthes biflora*	X	
Fabaceae	*Tephrosia florida*	X	
Fabaceae	*Trifolium dubium*	X	
Fabaceae	*Vicia acutifolia*	X	

Table A-1. Continued.

Family	Species	NPSpecies	This study
Fabaceae	*Vicia angustifolia*	X	
Fabaceae	*Vicia caroliniana*	X	
Fabaceae	*Vicia lathyroides*	X	
Fabaceae	*Vicia tetrasperma*	X	
Fabaceae	*Vigna luteola*	X	
Fabaceae	*Wisteria frutescens*	X	
Fabaceae	*Wisteria sinensis*	X	
Fabaceae	*Zornia bracteata*	X	
Fagaceae	*Castanea pumila*	X	
Fagaceae	*Quercus chapmanii*	X	
Fagaceae	*Quercus falcata*	X	
Fagaceae	*Quercus geminata*	X	X
Fagaceae	*Quercus hemisphaerica*	X	
Fagaceae	*Quercus incana*	X	
Fagaceae	*Quercus laevis*	X	
Fagaceae	*Quercus laurifolia*	X	X
Fagaceae	*Quercus maritima*	X	
Fagaceae	*Quercus myrtifolia*	X	X
Fagaceae	*Quercus nigra*	X	
Fagaceae	*Quercus stellata*	X	
Fagaceae	*Quercus virginiana*	X	X
Fumariaceae	*Corydalis micrantha*	X	
Gentianaceae	*Sabatia brachiata*	X	
Gentianaceae	*Sabatia stellaris*	X	
Geraniaceae	*Geranium carolinianum*	X	
Haloragaceae	*Myriophyllum aquaticum*	X	
Haloragaceae	*Proserpinaca pectinata*	X	
Hamamelidaceae	*Hamamelis virginiana*	X	
Hamamelidaceae	*Liquidambar styraciflua*	X	
Hippocastanaceae	*Aesculus pavia*	X	
Hydrocharitaceae	*Limnobium spongia*	X	X
Illiciaceae	*Illicium parviflorum*	X	
Iridaceae	*Hypoxis hirsuta*	X	
Iridaceae	*Sisyrinchium albidum*	X	
Iridaceae	*Sisyrinchium rosulatum*	X	
Juglandaceae	*Carya alba*	X	
Juglandaceae	*Carya glabra*	X	X
Juglandaceae	*Carya illinoinensis*	X	
Juncaceae	*Juncus acuminatus*	X	
Juncaceae	*Juncus bufonius*	X	
Juncaceae	*Juncus coriaceus*	X	
Juncaceae	*Juncus dichotomus*	X	
Juncaceae	*Juncus effusus*	X	

Table A-1. Continued.

Family	Species	NPSpecies	This study
Juncaceae	*Juncus marginatus*	X	
Juncaceae	*Juncus megacephalus*	X	
Juncaceae	*Juncus repens*	X	
Juncaceae	*Juncus roemerianus*	X	
Juncaceae	*Juncus scirpoides*	X	
Juncaceae	*Juncus tenuis*	X	
Juncaginaceae	*Triglochin striata*	X	
Lamiaceae	*Dicerandra linearifolia*	X	
Lamiaceae	*Dicerandra linearifolia var. linearifolia*	X	
Lamiaceae	*Leonotis nepetifolia*	X	
Lamiaceae	*Salvia coccinea*	X	
Lamiaceae	*Salvia lyrata*	X	
Lamiaceae	*Scutellaria integrifolia*	X	
Lamiaceae	*Stachys floridana*	X	
Lamiaceae	*Teucrium canadense*	X	
Lamiaceae	*Trichostema dichotomum*	X	
Lamiaceae	*Trichostema setaceum*	X	
Lauraceae	*Cinnamomum camphora*	X	
Lauraceae	*Persea borbonia*	X	X
Lauraceae	*Persea palustris*	X	
Lauraceae	*Sassafras albidum*	X	
Lemnaceae	*Landoltia punctata*	X	
Lemnaceae	*Lemna minor*	X	
Lemnaceae	*Lemna perpusilla*	X	
Lemnaceae	*Lemna valdiviana*	X	
Lemnaceae	*Spirodela polyrrhiza*	X	
Lemnaceae	*Wolffia columbiana*	X	
Lemnaceae	*Wolffiella gladiata*	X	
Lentibulariaceae	*Pinguicula pumila*	X	
Lentibulariaceae	*Utricularia cornuta*	X	
Lentibulariaceae	*Utricularia gibba*	X	
Lentibulariaceae	*Utricularia inflata*	X	
Lentibulariaceae	*Utricularia purpurea*	X	
Liliaceae	*Crinum asiaticum*	X	
Liliaceae	*Gloriosa superba*	X	
Liliaceae	*Narcissus tazetta*	X	
Liliaceae	*Nothoscordum bivalve*	X	
Linaceae	*Linum virginianum*	X	
Loganiaceae	*Gelsemium sempervirens*	X	X
Loganiaceae	*Mitreola petiolata*	X	
Loganiaceae	*Mitreola sessilifolia*	X	
Lygodiaceae	*Lygodium japonicum*	X	
Lythraceae	*Cuphea carthagenensis*	X	

Table A-1. Continued.

Family	Species	NPSpecies	This study
Lythraceae	*Decodon verticillatus*	X	X
Magnoliaceae	*Magnolia grandiflora*	X	
Magnoliaceae	*Magnolia virginiana*	X	
Magnoliaceae	*Michelia figo*	X	
Malvaceae	*Hibiscus grandiflorus*	X	
Malvaceae	*Hibiscus moscheutos*	X	
Malvaceae	*Kosteletzkya virginica*	X	
Malvaceae	*Sida acuta*	X	
Malvaceae	*Sida rhombifolia*	X	
Marantaceae	*Thalia dealbata*	X	
Marantaceae	*Thalia geniculata*	X	
Melastomataceae	*Rhexia mariana*	X	
Meliaceae	*Melia azedarach*	X	
Menyanthaceae	*Nymphoides aquatica*	X	
Molluginaceae	*Mollugo verticillata*	X	
Monotropaceae	*Monotropa uniflora*	X	
Moraceae	*Ficus pumila*	X	
Moraceae	*Morus rubra*	X	
Myricaceae	*Morella cerifera*	X	X
Najadaceae	*Najas marina*	X	
Nelumbonaceae	*Nelumbo lutea*	X	
Nyctaginaceae	*Boerhavia diffusa*	X	
Nymphaeaceae	*Nuphar luteum*	X	
Nymphaeaceae	*Nymphaea odorata*	X	
Nyssaceae	*Nyssa aquatica*	X	
Nyssaceae	*Nyssa sylvatica*	X	
Nyssaceae	*Nyssa sylvatica var. biflora*	X	X
Nyssaceae	*Nyssa sylvatica var. sylvatica*	X	
Oleaceae	*Chionanthus virginicus*	X	
Oleaceae	*Forestiera porulosa*	X	
Oleaceae	*Forestiera segregata*	X	
Oleaceae	*Ligustrum japonicum*	X	
Oleaceae	*Ligustrum lucidum*	X	
Oleaceae	*Olea europaea*	X	
Oleaceae	*Osmanthus americanus*	X	X
Onagraceae	*Gaura angustifolia*	X	
Onagraceae	*Ludwigia alata*	X	
Onagraceae	*Ludwigia alternifolia*	X	
Onagraceae	*Ludwigia arcuata*	X	
Onagraceae	*Ludwigia brevipes*	X	
Onagraceae	*Ludwigia leptocarpa*	X	
Onagraceae	*Ludwigia linearis*	X	
Onagraceae	*Ludwigia maritima*	X	

Table A-1. Continued.

Family	Species	NPSpecies	This study
Onagraceae	*Ludwigia palustris*	X	
Onagraceae	*Ludwigia suffruticosa*	X	
Onagraceae	*Oenothera humifusa*	X	
Onagraceae	*Oenothera laciniata*	X	
Onagraceae	*Oenothera speciosa*	X	
Ophioglossaceae	*Ophioglossum vulgatum*	X	
Orchidaceae	*Corallorrhiza wisteriana*	X	
Orchidaceae	*Epidendrum conopseum*	X	
Orchidaceae	*Habenaria repens*	X	
Orchidaceae	*Spiranthes praecox*	X	
Orchidaceae	*Spiranthes tuberosa*	X	
Orchidaceae	*Spiranthes vernalis*	X	
Orchidaceae	*Tipularia discolor*	X	
Orchidaceae	*Zeuxine strateumatica*	X	
Osmundaceae	*Osmunda cinnamomea*	X	
Osmundaceae	*Osmunda regalis*	X	X
Osmundaceae	*Osmunda regalis var. spectabilis*	X	
Oxalidaceae	*Oxalis corniculata*	X	
Oxalidaceae	*Oxalis corymbosa*	X	
Oxalidaceae	*Oxalis lyonii*	X	
Oxalidaceae	*Oxalis rubra*	X	
Oxalidaceae	*Oxalis stricta*	X	
Oxalidaceae	*Oxalis violacea*	X	
Papaveraceae	*Argemone albiflora*	X	
Papaveraceae	*Argemone mexicana*	X	
Passifloraceae	*Passiflora incarnata*	X	
Passifloraceae	*Passiflora lutea*	X	
Phytolaccaceae	*Phytolacca americana*	X	
Phytolaccaceae	*Phytolacca rigida*	X	
Pinaceae	*Cedrus deodara*	X	
Pinaceae	*Pinus elliottii*	X	X
Pinaceae	*Pinus glabra*	X	
Pinaceae	*Pinus palustris*	X	X
Pinaceae	*Pinus serotina*	X	X
Pinaceae	*Pinus taeda*	X	X
Plantaginaceae	*Plantago lanceolata*	X	
Plantaginaceae	*Plantago virginica*	X	
Platanaceae	*Platanus occidentalis*	X	
Plumbaginaceae	*Limonium carolinianum*	X	
Poaceae	*Andropogon glomeratus*	X	X
Poaceae	*Andropogon glomeratus var. glaucopsis*	X	
Poaceae	*Andropogon glomeratus var. glomeratus*	X	
Poaceae	*Andropogon ternarius*	X	
Poaceae	*Andropogon virginicus*	X	X

Table A-1. Continued.

Family	Species	NPSpecies	This study
Poaceae	*Andropogon virginicus var. virginicus*		X
Poaceae	*Aristida lanosa*	X	
Poaceae	*Aristida purpurascens*	X	
Poaceae	*Aristida purpurascens var. purpurascens*	X	
Poaceae	*Aristida purpurascens var. virgata*	X	
Poaceae	*Aristida stricta*		X
Poaceae	*Arundinaria gigantea*	X	
Poaceae	*Arundinaria tecta*	X	
Poaceae	*Arundo donax*	X	
Poaceae	*Axonopus compressus*	X	
Poaceae	*Axonopus fissifolius*	X	
Poaceae	*Axonopus furcatus*	X	X
Poaceae	*Bambusa glaucescens*	X	
Poaceae	*Bambusa tuldoides*	X	
Poaceae	*Briza minor*	X	
Poaceae	*Bromus catharticus*	X	
Poaceae	*Cenchrus echinatus*	X	
Poaceae	*Cenchrus longispinus*	X	
Poaceae	*Cenchrus spinifex*	X	
Poaceae	*Cenchrus tribuloides*	X	
Poaceae	*Chasmanthium laxum*	X	X
Poaceae	*Chasmanthium laxum var. sessiliflorum*	X	
Poaceae	*Chasmanthium sessiliflorum*	X	X
Poaceae	*Cynodon dactylon*	X	
Poaceae	*Dactyloctenium aegyptium*	X	
Poaceae	*Dichanthelium aciculare*	X	
Poaceae	*Dichanthelium commutatum*	X	
Poaceae	*Dichanthelium laxiflorum*	X	
Poaceae	*Dichanthelium portoricense*	X	
Poaceae	*Dichanthelium scabriusculum*	X	
Poaceae	*Dichanthelium spretum*	X	
Poaceae	*Dichanthelium strigosum var. leucoblepharis*	X	
Poaceae	*Dichanthelium wrightianum*	X	
Poaceae	*Digitaria ciliaris*	X	
Poaceae	*Digitaria sanguinalis*	X	
Poaceae	*Distichlis spicata*	X	X
Poaceae	*Echinochloa crus-galli*	X	
Poaceae	*Echinochloa muricata*	X	
Poaceae	*Echinochloa walteri*	X	
Poaceae	*Eleusine indica*	X	
Poaceae	*Eragrostis elliottii*	X	
Poaceae	*Eragrostis pectinacea*	X	
Poaceae	*Eragrostis pilosa*	X	

Table A-1. Continued.

Family	Species	NPSpecies	This study
Poaceae	*Eragrostis refracta*	X	
Poaceae	*Eragrostis secundiflora ssp. oxylepis*	X	
Poaceae	*Eragrostis spectabilis*	X	
Poaceae	*Eragrostis tenella*	X	
Poaceae	*Eremochloa ophiuroides*	X	X
Poaceae	*Eustachys glauca*	X	
Poaceae	*Eustachys petraea*	X	X
Poaceae	*Festuca subverticillata*	X	
Poaceae	*Lolium multiflorum*	X	
Poaceae	*Melica mutica*	X	
Poaceae	*Muhlenbergia capillaris*	X	
Poaceae	*Muhlenbergia capillaris var. filipes*	X	
Poaceae	*Muhlenbergia capillaris var. trichopodes*	X	
Poaceae	*Oplismenus hirtellus*	X	X
Poaceae	*Panicum acuminatum*	X	
Poaceae	*Panicum amarulum*	X	
Poaceae	*Panicum amarum*	X	
Poaceae	*Panicum anceps*	X	
Poaceae	*Panicum chamaelonche*	X	
Poaceae	*Panicum dichotomum*	X	
Poaceae	*Panicum hemitomon*	X	X
Poaceae	*Panicum oligosanthes var. oligosanthes*	X	
Poaceae	*Panicum portoricense*	X	
Poaceae	*Panicum rigidulum var. rigidulum*	X	
Poaceae	*Panicum verrucosum*	X	X
Poaceae	*Panicum virgatum*	X	X
Poaceae	*Paspalum dissectum*	X	
Poaceae	*Paspalum distichum*	X	
Poaceae	*Paspalum fluitans*	X	
Poaceae	*Paspalum notatum*	X	X
Poaceae	*Paspalum notatum var. saurae*	X	
Poaceae	*Paspalum setaceum*	X	
Poaceae	*Paspalum urvillei*	X	
Poaceae	*Paspalum vaginatum*	X	
Poaceae	*Phyllostachys aurea*	X	
Poaceae	*Piptochaetium avenaceum*	X	
Poaceae	*Poa annua*	X	
Poaceae	*Saccharum giganteum*	X	
Poaceae	*Sacciolepis striata*	X	
Poaceae	*Setaria faberi*	X	
Poaceae	*Setaria magna*	X	
Poaceae	*Setaria parviflora*	X	
Poaceae	*Sorghastrum nutans*	X	
Poaceae	*Sorghastrum secundum*	X	

Table A-1. Continued.

Family	Species	NPSpecies	This study
Poaceae	*Spartina alterniflora*	X	
Poaceae	*Spartina bakeri*	X	X
Poaceae	*Spartina patens*	X	
Poaceae	*Sphenopholis obtusata*	X	
Poaceae	*Sporobolus indicus*	X	
Poaceae	*Sporobolus teretifolius*	X	
Poaceae	*Sporobolus virginicus*	X	X
Poaceae	*Stenotaphrum secundatum*	X	
Poaceae	*Tridens flavus var. chapmanii*	X	
Poaceae	*Triplasis americana*	X	
Poaceae	*Triplasis purpurea*	X	
Poaceae	*Tripsacum dactyloides*	X	
Poaceae	*Uniola paniculata*	X	
Poaceae	*Urochloa platyphylla*	X	
Poaceae	*Vulpia myuros*	X	
Poaceae	*Vulpia octoflora*	X	
Polygalaceae	*Polygala grandiflora*	X	
Polygalaceae	*Polygala lutea*	X	
Polygonaceae	*Polygonella gracilis*	X	X
Polygonaceae	*Polygonum densiflorum*	X	
Polygonaceae	*Polygonum glaucum*	X	
Polygonaceae	*Polygonum hirsutum*	X	
Polygonaceae	*Polygonum hydropiperoides*	X	
Polygonaceae	*Polygonum punctatum*	X	
Polygonaceae	*Polygonum scandens var. cristatum*	X	
Polygonaceae	*Polygonum setaceum*	X	
Polygonaceae	*Rumex hastatulus*	X	
Polypodiaceae	*Phlebodium aureum*	X	
Polypodiaceae	*Pleopeltis polypodioides*	X	
Polypodiaceae	*Polypodium polypodioides*	X	
Pontederiaceae	*Pontederia cordata*	X	
Portulacaceae	*Portulaca oleracea*	X	
Portulacaceae	*Portulaca pilosa*	X	
Primulaceae	*Anagallis minima*	X	
Primulaceae	*Samolus parviflorus*	X	
Primulaceae	*Samolus valerandi*	X	
Ranunculaceae	*Clematis reticulata*	X	
Rhamnaceae	*Berchemia scandens*	X	
Rhamnaceae	*Frangula caroliniana*	X	
Rhamnaceae	*Sageretia minutiflora*	X	
Rosaceae	*Photinia pyrifolia*	X	
Rosaceae	*Prunus angustifolia*	X	
Rosaceae	*Prunus caroliniana*	X	

Family	Species	NPSpecies	This study
Rosaceae	*Prunus serotina*	X	X
Rosaceae	*Prunus serotina var. serotina*	X	
Rosaceae	*Prunus umbellata*	X	
Rosaceae	*Pyracantha koidzumii*	X	
Rosaceae	*Rubus argutus*	X	X
Rosaceae	*Rubus bifrons*	X	
Rosaceae	*Rubus cuneifolius*	X	
Rosaceae	*Rubus trivialis*	X	
Rubiaceae	*Cephalanthus occidentalis*	X	X
Rubiaceae	*Diodia teres*	X	X
Rubiaceae	*Diodia virginiana*	X	
Rubiaceae	*Galium hispidulum*	X	
Rubiaceae	*Galium obtusum*	X	
Rubiaceae	*Galium obtusum ssp. obtusum*	X	
Rubiaceae	*Galium obtusum var. obtusum*	X	
Rubiaceae	*Galium pilosum*	X	
Rubiaceae	*Houstonia procumbens*	X	
Rubiaceae	*Oldenlandia uniflora*	X	
Rubiaceae	*Pentodon pentandrus*	X	
Rubiaceae	*Richardia brasiliensis*	X	
Rubiaceae	*Richardia scabra*	X	
Ruppiaceae	*Ruppia maritima*	X	
Rutaceae	*Citrus aurantium*	X	
Rutaceae	*Citrus paradisi*	X	
Rutaceae	*Zanthoxylum clava-herculis*	X	X
Salicaceae	*Salix caroliniana*	X	X
Sapindaceae	*Sapindus marginatus*	X	
Sapotaceae	*Sideroxylon lycioides*	X	
Sapotaceae	*Sideroxylon tenax*	X	X
Saururaceae	*Saururus cernuus*	X	X
Scrophulariaceae	*Agalinis fasciculata*	X	
Scrophulariaceae	*Agalinis obtusifolia*	X	
Scrophulariaceae	*Agalinis purpurea*	X	
Scrophulariaceae	*Bacopa caroliniana*	X	
Scrophulariaceae	*Bacopa monnieri*	X	
Scrophulariaceae	*Buchnera americana*	X	
Scrophulariaceae	*Gratiola ramosa*	X	
Scrophulariaceae	*Micranthemum umbrosum*	X	
Scrophulariaceae	*Nuttallanthus canadensis*	X	
Scrophulariaceae	*Verbascum thapsus*	X	
Scrophulariaceae	*Veronica arvensis*	X	
Simaroubaceae	*Ailanthus altissima*	X	
Smilacaceae	*Smilax auriculata*	X	X
Smilacaceae	*Smilax bona-nox*	X	X

Table A-1. Continued.

Family	Species	NPSpecies	This study
Smilacaceae	Smilax glauca	X	X
Smilacaceae	Smilax laurifolia	X	X
Smilacaceae	Smilax pumila	X	
Smilacaceae	Smilax tamnoides	X	
Solanaceae	Datura stramonium	X	
Solanaceae	Lycium carolinianum	X	
Solanaceae	Physalis viscosa		X
Solanaceae	Physalis viscosa ssp. maritima	X	
Solanaceae	Physalis walteri	X	
Solanaceae	Solanum americanum	X	
Solanaceae	Solanum carolinense	X	
Solanaceae	Solanum pseudogracile	X	
Symplocaceae	Symplocos tinctoria	X	X
Tamaricaceae	Tamarix gallica	X	
Tamaricaceae	Tamarix parviflora	X	
Taxodiaceae	Taxodium ascendens	X	
Theaceae	Camellia japonica	X	
Theaceae	Gordonia lasianthus	X	
Thelypteridaceae	Thelypteris kunthii	X	
Thelypteridaceae	Thelypteris palustris	X	
Tiliaceae	Tilia americana var. heterophylla	X	
Tiliaceae	Triumfetta semitriloba	X	
Typhaceae	Typha angustifolia	X	
Typhaceae	Typha domingensis	X	
Typhaceae	Typha latifolia	X	
Ulmaceae	Celtis laevigata	X	
Ulmaceae	Celtis tenuifolia	X	
Ulmaceae	Ulmus americana	X	
Urticaceae	Boehmeria cylindrica	X	X
Urticaceae	Parietaria floridana	X	
Urticaceae	Pilea microphylla	X	
Urticaceae	Urtica chamaedryoides	X	
Verbenaceae	Callicarpa americana	X	
Verbenaceae	Glandularia pulchella	X	
Verbenaceae	Lantana ovatifolia	X	
Verbenaceae	Phyla nodiflora	X	X
Verbenaceae	Verbena scabra	X	
Violaceae	Viola brittoniana	X	
Violaceae	Viola lanceolata	X	
Violaceae	Viola palmata	X	
Violaceae	Viola septemloba	X	
Violaceae	Viola sororia	X	
Viscaceae	Phoradendron leucarpum	X	

Table A-1. Continued.

Family	Species	NPSpecies	This study
Vitaceae	*Ampelopsis arborea*	X	X
Vitaceae	*Parthenocissus quinquefolia*	X	X
Vitaceae	*Vitis aestivalis*	X	
Vitaceae	*Vitis aestivalis var. aestivalis*	X	
Vitaceae	*Vitis cinerea*	X	
Vitaceae	*Vitis cinerea var. cinerea*	X	
Vitaceae	*Vitis cinerea var. floridana*	X	
Vitaceae	*Vitis palmata*	X	
Vitaceae	*Vitis rotundifolia*	X	X
Vitaceae	*Vitis vulpina*	X	
Vittariaceae	*Vittaria lineata*	X	
Zamiaceae	*Zamia pumila*	X	
Zingiberaceae	*Alpinia zerumbet*	X	